(MOSTLY)
TRUE CONFESSIONS OF A
RECOVERING CATHOLIC

(MOSTLY)
TRUE CONFESSIONS OF A
RECOVERING CATHOLIC

Roger Neuhaus

iUniverse, Inc.
Bloomington

(MOSTLY) TRUE CONFESSIONS OF A RECOVERING CATHOLIC

iUniverse books may be ordered through booksellers or by contacting:

iUniverse
1663 Liberty Drive
Bloomington, IN 47403
www.iuniverse.com
1-800-Authors (1-800-288-4677)

ISBN: 978-1-4620-3489-5 (sc)
ISBN: 978-1-4620-3491-8 (hc)
ISBN: 978-1-4620-3490-1 (ebk)

Printed in the United States of America

iUniverse rev. date: 08/05/2011

CONTENTS

For my parents; Ken and Mary, my siblings; Mary Lynn, Patricia, Ken, Cathy, Tom, Greg and Paula, the Nevada Street neighborhood gang, and the friends, teachers and coaches at Nativity School who made my eight years there memorable enough to compel the writing of my first literary effort. And, of course, the City and people of Dubuque, Iowa—the best hometown in America.

—Roger Neuhaus—Tucson, Arizona. May 31, 2011

"I always wished I would have _____"

—Everyone

Dating back to my childhood days, I have always enjoyed telling stories that could entertain others, with the goal of seeking laughter. In my adult life, I have often shared these stories of youthful adventures about growing up in Dubuque, Iowa, with the people I have met in other parts of the country. After years of telling these same episodes to a variety of people in the different places I have lived over the years, it became apparent that some of them really resonated with folks. I also observed that my stories would prompt those I shared them with to draw on their own childhood experiences and share their stories with me in return.

Through these experiences, I have concluded that most people have a story or stories to tell, but rarely find the time or focus to bring them into recall or document them in any formal way. For about twenty years I had flirted with writing this book, but the needed inspiring moment finally hit me like a ton of bricks one summer afternoon in June of 2010 when my wife, Theresa, our younger son, Travis, and I attended a matinee comedy film titled Grown Ups. In short, the story line featured a group of fortyish-aged men who returned to their hometown, years after moving away, to attend the funeral of a former coach who had influenced their lives as boys. The reunion back in their hometown brings them to reminisce over a lot of humorous stories about people and events from their youth. As Theresa, Travis and I left the theater on that hot Tucson afternoon I told them that if what we just watched could attract millions of people to the theater, then I could certainly write something relating my own stories, that could also serve to entertain others and perhaps inspire them to pass their own stories on.

Thus, an author was born.

I want to express my thanks and appreciation to the following people who encouraged the completion of this work through their willingness to critique my ideas, listen to me read through some of the draft material, or peruse it on their own. My younger brother Greg, the real artist in my family, who was the first to read Chapter One and who challenged me with something to the effect of "Those are one thousand pretty good words, only ninety thousand more to go. What else ya got"? Theresa, Travis and my older son, Aaron, who listened to my ramblings on and off throughout the summer of 2010 as the book began to come together, providing feedback on what was good and what needed some refining. Then Art Worthington, who listened to a few of the early chapters over a cold Coors or two when we visited at his cabin at Twin Lakes, near Yosemite National Park, over the fourth of July weekend. Rich and Maggie Tyler, on their back patio in East Dubuque, Illinois in late July, amid a good old fashioned mid-western thunderstorm. Kathy and Dave Schaller when they visited Tucson in January of 2011, and prompted me to get back to some final edits that were overdue. Dr. Scott Klewer, who heals young hearts at the Steele Children's Research Center and University of Arizona College of Medicine in Tucson, but applied his gentle bedside manner often when I needed someone to listen, laugh, and call for more. Thanks as well are due Autumn Conley for the original comprehensive edit, and my sister, M.L., for the final edit.

INTRODUCTION

The audience this book is likely to resonate with includes millions of Baby Boomers who grew up in the Catholic faith, particularly, but not exclusively, those who no longer practice, and anyone who grew up in a large family or during the time period in which the stories are told.

The themes have to do with the changing times that occurred during the era referenced, struggles with the dichotomy of much misbehavior within a highly structured and disciplined environment, nostalgic references to the way things were in a simpler time and place, and ultimately, confessions of misdeeds that were often covered up, concealed, and withheld from authority figures. The happenings and characters in this book are, to the best of the author's recall, close to the reality of the time, with a sprinkling of embellishments added sparingly for dramatic effect.

AUTHOR BIOGRAPHY

Roger Neuhaus grew up as the sixth of eight children in the 1960's and 1970's in the predominantly Catholic Midwestern town of Dubuque, Iowa—a community of some 55,000 residents located on the banks of the Mississippi River at the eastern edge of the state. His early years were heavily influenced by the teachings of the Catholic grade school and church that were at the center of his family's core values. Since stepping away from the Catholic Church during his teenage years, he has enjoyed exposure to a variety of different faiths, while maintaining respect for the culture that defined his youth. Though his life's journey has afforded him the opportunity to live in a cross-section of American cities and towns, including Cedar Falls and Iowa City in Iowa, Chicago and Carbondale in Illinois, Los Angeles in California, and Phoenix, Flagstaff, Cottonwood, Tucson and Payson in Arizona, Neuhaus acknowledges the Middle American values nurtured during his childhood as the inspiration behind his life's work of fundraising on behalf of not-for-profit organizations. He resides in Tucson and Payson, Arizona with Theresa, his high school sweetheart and wife of twenty-five years, and their sons, Aaron and Travis.

CHAPTER 1

First Recall

I grew up in Dubuque, population 50,000-something, in the northeast section of the great State of Iowa, on the banks of the Mississippi River where the Hawkeye state, Illinois, and Wisconsin seek unsuccessfully to connect. It was the 1960's and 1970's. Things were simple, and people treated one another like family. Summers were sticky and humid and packed with adventure; winters were frigid and too long; the fade of autumn was sad; and the first signs of spring inspiring.

It was a time when color television was the newest technology, the hula hoop was the latest fad, the first videogame (Pong) was yet to be introduced, and the evening news typically began with coverage of American soldiers fighting a misunderstood war in a faraway land called Vietnam. All in all, life was resoundingly good in Dubuque. Of course, back then, we had nothing to compare it to.

The earliest memory I can recall about being the sixth of eight children in a Catholic school and church-going family, was in the basement of my family home at 116 Nevada Street, commonly referred to by my siblings and me simply as '116'. It was a mid-October day in 1965 or '66 at 116. Ken Neuhaus had fathered eight children in the first eleven years of marriage to his wife Mary (don't let the 'holy' name fool ya, as there was nothing immaculate about these undeniably Catholic conceptions) and now spent most of his days and nights working multiple jobs to feed them. He had driven to his day job at the loading dock of Torbert Drug Company that morning in the baby blue 1962 Buick family station wagon—the kind with a rumble seat facing out the back. The rumble seat was a favored place in the car, and inevitably, three of the eight Neuhaus offspring fought over it on family drives; apparently, there was something alluring about inhaling the carbon dioxide fumes that crept in the window as we tooled along. The sun was bright, pretending to be warm, but the cool wind that blew that morning kept my younger brother Greg and me playing in the house instead of outdoors.

In the basement of the house, a musty aroma always prevailed amidst the limestone block walls and hard concrete floors. I must have been about four years old, and Greg was about two. We were playing together, but kind of doing our own separate things as we passed the hours. While we awaited the greater excitement that came with the older kids returning home from school, I decided to play a trick on Greg and see what kind of reaction it would bring. In retrospect, it was a really poor decision on my part. Like so many other things that go awry in life, it seemed like a good idea at the time and turned out to be anything but.

As Greg played on the floor with the contents of Dad's tin red toolkit strewn around him, I approached him from behind with an illuminated flashlight pointed upward from below my chin. In such a sparsely lit area, the distortion of my face proved a bit unnerving. In the scariest voice a four-year-old could muster, I began to tell Greg I was a ghost. He verbalized his belief that it was just I, but he began to tremble, trying to convince himself of what he was saying. I persisted with my act and expounded that I was actually the ghost of Roger because I had killed the real Roger and was now about to kill him. Apparently, Greg did not feel his young life should be over just yet, so in a reactive motion of self-defense, the resourceful and terrified toddler lifted a ball pin hammer from the tool kit, raised it over his head with both hands, and brought it down on my forehead with a force I had seen only one other time in a coyote and roadrunner cartoon on TV.

Boooom! Down like Jack from the beanstalk went the ghost of Roger, who, as it turns out, must have known our mother somehow, because he ran up the basement stairs instinctively while frantically screaming for her as he held his hands over his nose, now gushing bright red blood from both nostrils. Perhaps it's not such a good idea to back even the smallest of opponents into a corner. Thus, the first of many life lessons I can recall learning the hard way during my tenure at 116.

CHAPTER 2

Let it Snow

Our place at 116 was poised on the corner of Nevada and Solon Streets. It was a large white three-story home that was raised on a natural grassy terrace about fifteen feet above street level. It sat prominently in its place, appearing somewhat more stately than most of the middle—to lower-middle-class abodes in the neighborhood, mostly due to its elevated status and a large, long limestone block wall that skirted the entire front of the house like a mote protecting a castle along the Solon Street front entrance.

A favorite way of entertaining ourselves during the cold and snowy winters of the era involved my three brothers and me, a handful of other available neighbor boys, and the pliability of a heavy, wet snow that allowed for the effortless reshaping of a flat layer of the glistening white stuff into softball-sized projectiles. With a simple scoop and cupping of the hands, a couple of pats, and a little smooth shaping of the edges . . . behold, a weapon was born. One Saturday evening around the middle of January, a group of us were looking up enjoying the backdrop of a dark winter sky and the reflection of the moonlight off the swirling, featherlike snowflakes as they fell from above. We were involved in a heated competition to see who could catch the most flakes on their tongue. After this exercise lost its appeal, we began to seek other ways to entertain ourselves. It was a good, wet snow, and as we pondered what else could be done with it, there was only one logical answer: It was the perfect occasion to take target practice at the occasional slowly passing automobiles.

About six of us took our positions, mostly on the terrace and behind the trees on the elevated snow-covered yard that surrounded 116 on the Nevada Street side. We each prepared two snowballs, one for each hand. We stood motionless in the damp winter silence, waiting for headlights to appear from the end of the block that would announce the unsuspecting next victim. As a car approached, we cocked our respective throwing arms back and fired the first round of attack mortars, flipping the others to our throwing hands like a second baseman dropping the ball from his glove to turn a double play and then firing to first. In the course of about five seconds, the passing motorist received ten to twelve sudden and alarming *thumps* to their windshield, hoods, and doors. The immediate reaction of each passing motorist would be a sudden slamming of their brakes, which would cause their car to slide on the snow-packed asphalt, followed by relief when they could regain control of the car and pass on down the block. It wasn't until then that they realized they had been on the receiving end of a prank. Occasionally, a pounded car stopped momentarily, as if the driver was considering getting out and pursuing his or her attackers, but they never really wanted to leap from a warm car out into the cold Iowa night to hunt down a band of deviants who had really caused no significant damage . . . at least not until Polka Dots showed up.

CHAPTER 3

Frank and John's

From about 1968 until 1975, the Neuhaus brothers staked claim to and retained ownership of the neighborhood paper route. Yes, Route 155 of <u>The Dubuque Telegraph-Herald</u> was in good hands back then. The papers were delivered reliably and on time for the better part of those seven years. As anyone who managed a paper route during that era knows, every route had a drop location where the newspaper truck would leave the bundled stack of papers at the same place and time each day for the carriers to pick up, place in their canvas bags, and hand deliver to the customers' doors. Route 155 consisted of ninety-eight doors, and the drop location for the route was at a place called Frank and John's Gulf Station—a neighborhood filling and auto repair garage. Of course, this was back in the day before convenience stores became the norm. Our papers were dropped outside on the step of the station near the metal refrigerated box that contained ice for sale. Rarely did a day pass that did not find us inside the lobby of the station with our eyes gazing longingly through the glass encased counter that contained more varieties of confections than anyone could ever eat. There were Rolos, Three Musketeers, Milky Ways, Snickers, Zagnuts,

Mambo Pies, Zero bars, Nougats, Snirkels, Black Jack chewing gum, Charms suckers, and more. Across the lobby against the wall on the path to the restroom was a soda machine with a big 7-up logo on it that read THE UNCOLA. It had a six-inch wide clear glass door that ran from top to bottom of the machine on the right-hand side. Through the glass, we could see twelve different sodas stacked horizontally atop one another, separated by individual metal circles around each bottle. Back then, instead of buttons, we had to look at the bottle cap we saw through the glass door, and for ten cents, we could open the glass door and pull the bottle from its metal circle and another one would fall from somewhere else into its place, as though it had always been there. Infinite sodas? What a concept!

Frank and John's had a distinct character about it. The aroma that greeted us when we entered the twelve-by-twelve lobby was something of a hearty mixture of oil, gasoline, and the rubber from tires and windshield wiper replacement blades all rolled into one. There was a calendar on the wall behind the counter that was supposedly an advertisement for NAPA auto parts, but, being the pre-pubescent hormone factories we were, we were more impressed by the luscious blonde who occupied most of it than by air filters and car batteries. She had sexy little pigtails, bright red lipstick, skimpy cut-offs that left little to the imagination, and a tank top with lots of cleavage spilling out. If auto repair can be suggestive, the calendar had accomplished it, as she was holding a dipstick in her hand and wiping it off with a cloth as if there was nothing in the world she would rather be doing. We all decided that we wanted to buy our auto parts at her store when we got our first cars!

The linoleum square-tiled floor had a permanent smear of black grease embedded in most of it, and every time a car pulled into the gas lane and ran over an air hose that was stretched across the drive, a bell would ding twice to alert the guys in the auto repair bay that a customer had arrived.

Perhaps the most distinct thing about Frank and John's persona, however, were the guys who worked there. They were a surly bunch of grease monkeys, if you will. We were pretty sure none of them ever finished high school (if they even made it that far), had ever taken a bath, had ever seen a dentist, or would ever get the grease out from under their fingernails. One thing that we knew for certain was that none of them were ever going to get a date with the pretty girl on the calendar despite the cool shirts they wore with their nicknames scripted above the pocket. There were Frank and John George, an uncle and nephew who were the proprietors. Frank wore the full Gulf Station uniform, with matching navy Dickies slacks and shirt. He must have been the senior partner. There was John McCann, the guy most of us recognized more by his ass crack than his face because of his proclivity for always being bent over at the waist with his head under the hood of a car, and his jeans hanging way too low. Colby was about five-three and 250 pounds, and he had three or four chins; he clearly spent too much time with his head in the glass confection counter out front.

And then, there was Polka Dots. We called him 'Polka Dots' because while all the guys at the station wore some type of hat that was auto related, he opted for a pink one with white polka dots. We didn't know how he got away with this among his co-workers, but he did. It was unreal.

CHAPTER 4

Polka Dots and Harpo

As the next car approached that snowy January evening, my brothers, the neighborhood guys, and I had shuffled our positions a bit. It had been a while since a car had come, so we got impatient and had begun a snowball fight amongst ourselves. As someone yelled out "CAR!" we all scooped for snow to reload for an assault on the approaching vehicle. Just at the moment the white arsenal began to fly, I quickly realized that during the position shift, I had ended up below the grade of the yard at 116, very near the sidewalk on Nevada Street, about ten feet from the car that had now slammed on its brakes and had been thrown into park in what appeared to be one fluid instant. It was not a mere veiled threat. This driver was actually braving the arctic temperatures to get out and come after us. In the darkness of the evening, his bright fluorescent hat was unmistakable. "Holy shit! Polka Dots!"

As everyone turned and ran through the yard at 116 to escape the area by ducking into an alley, I found myself in a losing attempt at sprinting up the middle of Solon Street. I had received a pair of knee-high army green colored rubber boots for Christmas a few weeks earlier, and up until that moment in time, I thought they were pretty cool. But on this fateful night, what I really needed were some PF flyers. As I got about halfway up Solon Street and near the end of a wooden fence that corralled the yard of the house across the street from ours, I decided to try and make a quick turn around the corner of the fence to escape into another yard. As I began to round the fence, I peered over my shoulder to check on the progress of Polka Dots: He was on my ass and not letting up. As I turned my head forward again, out of the darkness a telephone pole appeared two-steps in front of me. I bolted to the right to dodge it, but slipped on the incline of a snow bank, falling onto my back with a *thud*. The next thing I knew, Polka Dots had me pinned to the frozen ground and was sitting on my chest, rubbing icy cold snow in my face and stuffing it in my stocking cap and pulling it down over my eyes. The whole time—which seemed like an eternity—he was cursing violently, a selection of lingo he had obviously taken from Frank and John's potty-mouth dictionary that Sister Mary Paschal at Nativity School had told us would make us go to hell. Mercifully, the wrath of Polka Dots subsided eventually. I suppose he realized he had ventured some distance from his running car, which was blocking the street that had been narrowed to one lane due to the blizzard conditions. As he turned away, I arose from the snow bank and began to empty the snow from my stocking cap. It was then that another life lesson was bestowed upon me: Don't mess with people who dress like they're crazy, because they probably are. But in Polka Dots' case, at least there was justice in knowing he was going to hell anyway. Sister Mary Paschal said so.

While Polka Dots was a strange character indeed, he was certainly not the most eccentric guy wandering around Dubuque back in the day. That esteemed title would have to go to a guy by the name of Harpo.

Nearly two decades before Madonna came on to the pop scene and made one-word names fashionable, Harpo was already onto it. Perhaps, then-popular Sonny or Cher inspired him, but whatever the reason, Harpo kept his first and surnames hidden from public knowledge. He was just Harpo . . . and God only made one of him.

Harpo lived downtown at a place called the Iowa Inn, which had previously served for many years as the YMCA. When a new Y was built, the Iowa Inn evolved into some type of government-subsidized housing project. The rooms were similar to dorms at an old college, with common shower and toilet areas. The Iowa Inn was, in essence, the last line of defense against homelessness, and for Harpo, it served a much-needed purpose.

Harpo had a number of distinguishing characteristics. He stood about six-two and weighed a slight 110 or 120 pounds. He rode a bicycle with dual baskets on the back and a tall orange stick with a caution flag that stuck out of one of the baskets, ascending about six feet in the air. When he got off the bike, he walked with a pronounced limp, caused by one leg being about four inches shorter than the other. One side of his face and neck was about three times bigger than the other due to a massive goiter that was quite visible and seemed to have grown bigger each time we saw him. He wore Coke-bottle-thick eyeglasses and always—and I mean ALWAYS—sported a faded old light blue Chicago Cubs cap with his long, black, greasy, stringy hair falling out from under it to his shoulders. The hat had the trademark block letter C on the front, and he tilted it slightly off center, which may have symbolized something greater. Whenever anyone encountered Harpo, it was almost predictable that he would slur the same phrase: "Cub it up." Those who found themselves on the receiving end of the seemingly pre-recorded greeting would repeat the phrase back to him: "Yeah, Cub it up, Harp." That was the extent of most of Harpo's conversations, and the same thing was spoken nearly every time for years and years on end.

Above all that distinguished Harpo as the most unique local ambassador downtown Dubuque would ever know was his fascination—or obsession, I suppose—with collecting burned-out florescent light bulbs. These objects of his affection were long and tubular, white, about three inches in diameter, and four to six feet long, and the collection of them was his thing, his occupation. He spent his days riding his bike up and down the streets, stopping at every merchant and commercial or public business with open doors to ask if they had any of the burned-out treasures. They often had bulbs to give him, and just about every time anyone saw the man, he had at least two or more of them sticking out toward the sky from each basket of his bike. No one knew for sure what he did with the bulbs or where he stored them, but we all knew he collected lots of them. That was for certain.

Years later, when I was in the eighth grade, one of our teachers/coaches at Nativity, Mike Cosgrove, who had gone to high school with Harpo, told us his real name was Ray something-or-other and that he took too many drugs as a teenager, which resulted in his limited abilities and odd behavior. We all made a note at that point to avoid drugs should anyone ever offer them to us. We had higher hopes for our futures than collecting light bulbs on our bicycles.

CHAPTER 5

Hot Wheels Track

We didn't always play outside during the winter. In fact, we spent a good deal of time on winter weekends inventing our own fun in the basement at 116. Saturday was the proclaimed shopping and cleaning day. After several hours of the kids being plopped in front of the Magnavox television watching morning cartoons, Mary would arrive home from grocery shopping at a place called the Warehouse Market. She always brought home cardboard boxes—no "Paper or plastic?" in those days—of everything that was on sale that week. The Warehouse Market was really little more than a mass distribution center for cheap wholesale food and household items. It had sealed concrete floors throughout, and the walls were made of beige-colored, waffled sheet metal. It was warm in the summer and cold in the winter. The grocery carts were not metal baskets on wheels, but rather large rectangular hardwood skids with heavy green bars on one end to steer them, and iron wheels akin to what you might find on . . . well, nothing else; they were just big, unbreakable iron wheels. The target market for this store consisted of middle—to lower-middle-class families of eight to fourteen, stuck on a tight food budget. We most definitely fell into that category and ate our share of peanut butter, pancake mix, cereal, bread, canned soup, Jenos make-your-own-pizza-at-home kits, and off-brand foods with strange names like Happy's Potato Chips, which featured a big smiling clown face on the front of the box and had two plastic pouches of chips inside. If that wasn't fun eatin', Polka Dots wasn't bound for hell! Shasta was the soda of choice at the Warehouse because it was only eleven cents per can and we could pick and choose from a variety of tasty flavors. Regardless of what was purchased, it was guaranteed to be cheap and plentiful. That was the Warehouse way, and Mary loved it.

As she entered the house from shopping, Mary yelled, "Let's get you strong boys out here to carry in some groceries! Then we've got some housecleaning to do." We always went along with her requests for two reasons: One, we wanted to go through the boxes to see what good stuff was there and then try to hide it from our siblings for our own munching later; and two, if we didn't respond, we would get the Hot Wheels track. The latter of these reasons tended to be the most persuasive.

One year, for his birthday, my brother Tom (two years older than me) had received a package of tiny cars with movable wheels. The package had a Mattel logo, and the cars were called Hot Wheels. They were all the rage as far as boys were concerned, and Tom began to collect a variety of the various cool body types that mimicked some of the neatest real car designs of the time, like the Chevy Camaro, Ford Mustang, Dodge Charger, Mercury Cougar, and others. After he had collected enough of the cars, he went on a quest for more and more sections of the pliable orange plastic track the cars ran on. Each section of track was about two feet long and two inches wide, and multiple pieces could be connected to make a longer and longer track—even loops and competitive downhill parallel tracks to race cars against one another. One day, when Mary had reached her limit with my brother Ken for one reason or another (Ken, five years my senior, was never at a loss for providing plenty of reason), she began to chase him through the house, but could not get within arm's reach to give him what she deemed the necessary smack. Tom was there, playing with his Hot Wheels, and as Mary dashed by him in hot pursuit of Ken, without breaking stride, she swiped a piece of the orange track from Tom and swung it at our brother, catching the back of his leg. Ken let out a shriek that could be heard down the block. Our mother had pretty much lost her ability to intimidate us by that point, but with the introduction of the Hot Wheels track as the newest weapon in her disciplinary arsenal, Mary once again had our attention. Soon thereafter, we begged of Tom that he hide his track pieces when he was done playing with them, someplace where our mother could not find them in a fit of rage. She was smarter than we thought. She ended up confiscating one piece of the nasty track and found her own hiding place for it, and from that day forward, she didn't hesitate to whip it out when she meant business.

CHAPTER 6

Oh No, Big Bro

My brother Ken was the oldest boy in the family, the third oldest child. I don't know what compels a father to give one of his sons his own name and place 'Jr.' on the end of it, but from observing the relationship between my father and his designated junior—and more importantly, the arrogant and dictatorial actions on my brother's part that seemed to correlate with the sharing of our father's name—I made a note to never do that to one of my sons if I were ever to have any. I was certain Webster would define the word 'bully' with a picture of my brother Ken. There was a hit television show in the late 1980s and early 1990s called <u>The Wonder Years</u>, and Ken was the spitting image of lead character Kevin's older brother Wayne. 'Butthead' is too kind of a description.

An example of Ken's emperor-like behavior can be illustrated with a little tidbit about a favorite activity that went on amongst the boys in the Nevada Street neighborhood back in the late 1960's: the building and racing of go-karts. We all read in <u>Boy's Life</u> and <u>Sports Illustrated</u> magazines about the infamous annual soap box derby that was conducted as a national competition each summer, and we dreamed of racing in it. Various groups of boys in the area where we lived assembled teams that would build, maintain, and push the manually powered cars around the neighborhood. The cars consisted, in large part, of a two-inch thick, six-foot long board that served as the chassis. A couple of two-by-fours were connected in the front and back to function as axles. We removed wheels from little red wagons and attached them, with over-sized cotter pins, to the axles of our carts. The front axle had to have a bolt connected to the chassis, centered in the middle, to allow the driver to steer the front axle with his feet.

After the various teams had built their carts, perhaps five or six in total, we challenged one another to meet at one of the many hills in the area to compete for the area soapbox derby championship. Ken always insisted on driving our cart and summoned his team, Tom and me included, to drag the cart by a rope that attached to the front axle to and from the hilly locations where the races were run. When the downhill race ended, the overworked crew, but never the holier-than-thou driver, had to pull the cart back up the hill. The outcomes of the competitions were typically judged on the best performance in two of three or three of five races. As a result, the car had to be pulled back up the steep course between three and five times. Never once did Ken lend a hand, but he was always quick to reclaim the makeshift racecar when it had reached the top of the hill, just in time to line up for the next race. As the summer racing series wore on, the crew grew weary of doing all the required maintenance on the cart, dragging it to race locations, and pulling it up the course multiple times each day to satisfy Ken's unjustified demands. Eventually, the crew began to dwindle in numbers, having lost interest in what had become the predictable monotony of their drone existence.

During the years when Ken was the proprietor of Route 155 for The Telegraph-Herald newspaper, after having served his time as an indentured slave to Johnny Welter, the previous franchise owner, who had graduated to part-time pump attendant at Frank and John's Gulf Station, Tom and I served as his labor force. Ken assigned us to deliver to the houses that required many steps be climbed to reach their mailboxes; the houses that required calculated dashes between cars speeding across Dodge Street; and the homes that housed residents who didn't clear their snow-packed and icy sidewalks in the winter. The Almighty One even found it convenient to take an off day and leave the entire delivery to his subservient carriers on Wednesdays, when all of the merchant sale inserts were stuffed in the center of the papers, thus increasing the weight of the canvas carrying bags by about three times compared to other days. Perhaps Ken's greatest moment as a tyrant dictator, however, was the day he decided to test out a Christmas gift on us before it was time.

One Saturday afternoon in the winter of 1970, Ken, Tom, Greg, and I were hanging out in the basement of 116. Santa had been gracious enough to send Ken one of those pump-action pellet guns for Christmas, but he was told he could not use it until it was warm enough to go outside and shoot it in the spring. If my brother Ken understood anything in life, it was that rules were intended for everyone except him. Disregarding our parents' directive about use of the gun in the house, Ken suggested a game whereby he would load the pellet gun, pump it about fifteen or twenty times, increasing the firing velocity of the pellet to be discharged with each pump, as Tom, Greg, and I put on football helmets and dashed across the basement floor, taking cover behind the three one-foot square crossbeams that held the house up. The lunatic demanded that we run back and forth for our lives while he took wild shots at us until someone was hit. The game ended only when Tom was hit in the back and let out a wail that Mary could hear from upstairs.

When our mother came downstairs to see what was going on, the gig was up. She disappeared momentarily and returned with her trusty Hot Wheels track. Run for your lives! The lesson learned on this fine day was that the oldest child—even if he has your Dad's name—is not necessarily the most cerebral.

CHAPTER 7

Gasoline Alley and More

Most of the neighborhood blocks in the thirty-or-so-square block area that comprised our extended turf between Dodge Street and University Avenue and Booth and Hill Streets had alleys that were carved down the middle of them, splitting the blocks in half. Many homes had garages in back that were accessed by way of the alleys. The mostly gravel-based and occasionally brick byways also provided routes for the City of Dubuque garbage trucks to pick up trash containers residents stored behind their homes in order to maximize curb appeal. For us, the alleys became alternative play areas and were great for shortcuts whether we were on foot or bikes.

We passed many a summer day standing in the gravel alley behind 116, scooping nickel—and quarter-sized pieces of gravel, tossing them in the air, and hitting them as far up the alley as we could with various makeshift bats constructed from broken tree branches or old wooden handles from discarded rakes or shovels. A lot of stray rocks hit garages and landed in neighboring yards, and from time to time, we were suspended from play for a week or two due to complaints received by our parents from unhappy neighbors.

But ultimately, batting rocks was too much fun to resist, and the games resumed after a brief sabbatical.

Winter brought new uses for the alleyways. Few vehicles braved the alleys that spanned from Langworthy Street to Dodge Street during the winter months because they were not plowed or maintained by the salt trucks that took care of the regular streets. This made them prime sledding grounds for us, and we did lots of sledding. Every kid in the area had a Flexible Flyer or Yankee Clipper sled, and when the alleys got good and packed with ice and snow, we waxed up the metal runners and hit the slopes. We always started at Langworthy, proceeded down the alley to Solon Street, crossed Solon, and continued all the way down to Dodge Street, without interruption. The total course was probably about 300 yards of gradually increasing slope north to south, until the last 50 yards dropped off with a dramatic decline that provided a great finishing rush. At night, we rolled up old newspapers, soaked them in gasoline, positioned them strategically and intermittently down the center of the course, and raced down the alley on our sleds, lighters in hand, to see who could successfully light the most torches while flying by on our sleds. The lit papers burned for about five minutes and brightened the path for the walk back up to the top to prepare for another run.

One of the neighborhood soapbox derby teams we raced against was Team Chapman, which consisted primarily of the three Chapman brothers—Gene, Gary ('Boog'), and Greg ('Little Boog')—as well as a handful of on-again/off-again crewmembers.

The Chapmans lived a stone's toss up the alley behind 116, the one that connected Langworthy and Solon Streets. The alley provided access to their garage, but their cars were always parked on Langworthy Street . . . all except for one, that is. Not only did the Chapmans race soapbox derby cars, but also they had a real orange and white stock car that occupied their garage. Gene Sr. entered it in the weekly Sunday-night stock car races during the summer season at the Dubuque County Fairgrounds dirt track. It was the Chapman's pride and joy, and from May until the end of September, the object of their constant obsession, oftentimes to the dismay of residents who lived within four or five blocks of the place.

Three or four nights per week, all summer long and often well into the evening hours when many folks were trying to sleep, the Chapman's tinkered in their garage, door open, working on the obnoxiously loud car, which had no muffler to soften its engine noise. The engine ran for hours, with regular revving that caused a series of backfires that would send any shell-shocked Vietnam veteran into instant flashback mode. This went on for at least ten or twelve years.

With all the work that went into the Chapman's car, one would assume that they must have had the mean machine primed to win some races come Sunday nights, but that was hardly the case. As young boys, my brothers and I used to attend the races on occasion because Dad, with his Sheriff's gig, worked security at the races on his own time for extra money. A fringe benefit was that all his kids got in to the events for free. As we sat in the dust-filled, deafening grandstand during the races, two things were guaranteed: One, by the time the races were over for the evening, our ears would be ringing; and two, the Chapman's orange and white car would have broken down, caught fire, been the cause of a debilitating collision, or driven off the track and down over the hill on the back stretch. We joked that they alone kept the Beidler Brothers' Wrecker Service in business. If Team Chapman ever finished a race, it was considered a moral victory. The end product of the toil that went on all week in their garage was not worth anyone losing the sleep over it, though everyone in the neighborhood did.

Team Chapman, the soapbox derby division, had several on-again/off-again crewmembers, the most colorful being Kevin Ryan. Kevin was nicknamed 'Craze' by the insensitive boys in the neighborhood because he suffered from some type of mental illness, which, back in the day, was just thrown into the broad label of being crazy. Kevin clearly had some emotional issues, including a raging temper that occasionally made him violent toward others. He also had a real foot fetish and worshipped the bare feet of the girls on the block, who rarely wore shoes in the summer time. In addition,

Kevin had some type of fascination with Cavalry and Civil War figures and often dressed and acted the part. The boy was certainly strange.

Instead of being sympathetic or helpful to Kevin, we tended to pick on, ridicule, and razz him so we could be entertained by his predictably bizarre reactions. To really freak him out when he rode his bike near where we hung out, our whole gang would jump on our bikes and pursue him, yelling threats. Kevin, always wearing cowboy boots and a Western or Civil War outfit, pumped his bike pedals with greater and greater urgency, all the while panting and looking back over his shoulder as the pack of mini-Hells Angels closed the gap on him. In retrospect, one may argue we were the crazy ones.

When Kevin's issues became very bad, he would disappear for a few months. We later learned he was sent for occasional stays at an institution, where he presumably received electroshock therapy, counseling, and the latest medications the pharmaceutical industry was developing and testing on the population it would later be prescribed for. When he returned from these junkets, he temporarily showed some clear signs of improvement. His temper seemed more controlled, he was more conversational and less detached, and he exhibited behavior that showed he was aware of some things that needed to be overcome. Being children, who have a propensity for being cruel and truly thoughtless, upon the early phase of one of Kevin's returns from a trip away, we decided to test him to see if we could set him off. Lord, what were we thinking?

The Walsh Store was a favorite retail outlet we would ride our bikes to in the summer months. It was downtown on Central Avenue, and it was a fixture for all things juvenile. The third floor was the toy/game floor, and they had anything and everything a kid could want. Something we always enjoyed buying were peashooters. The peashooter itself was nothing more than an overly sturdy and slightly larger version of a red-and-white-striped straw like the kind you might get at the drive-in when you bought a thick milkshake. The shooters came in a pack of two, one yellow and one white, with a four-ounce paper pouch of little white beans. You could buy extra bags of the beans, and we did. The concept was that you would fill your mouth with a dozen or so of the small beans, place the tip of the shooter in your mouth, and then blow the beans through the shooter in spitfire succession. We used them as weapons to fire at one another, and as far as we were concerned, it was good stuff.

As our way of welcoming Kevin home from his latest vacation, we returned from the Walsh Store with our shooters and plenty of extra bags of ammo. About six of us laid on our bellies on the slight terrace that rose upward from the sidewalk to Ryan's front porch. We positioned ourselves, mocking the way we had seen U.S. soldiers do it in television shows and in movies when they prepared to wage an ambush assault upon the enemy.

The Ryan's residence on Alpine Street, just up the alley from 116, had a big wooden Victorian-style wrap-around porch that dressed the front of the house. Slightly raised off the porch-level entrance to the house was an oversized glass picture window that measured about eight or ten feet square. We took our positions, filled our mouths with the rock-hard white beans, and on the count of three, we all aimed and fired about fifty or sixty beans at the glass target in unison. A prolonged series of *clings, clangs* and *tinks* ensued as our beans bounced off the window, followed by a series of clicking noises as they bounced about the wooden porch floor. We reloaded, aimed, and spit-fired again, emptying hundreds of rounds in the course of just a few minutes, littering the porch with the spent debris.

As we prepared to reload for the fifth or sixth time, the front door opened, and out stepped Kevin, holding a large boiling pot in one hand and a wooden stirring spoon in the other. Had we gotten him to crack already? No. Much to our surprise, using the spoon as a shovel, Kevin scooped up all of the beans off the porch and into the pot. As we looked on in stunned amazement, Kevin turned to us before stepping calmly back into the house and said, "Thanks for the beans, fellas. I'm going to make a big pot of soup with them, and you're all invited back in about an hour for a soup dinner."

We all looked at each other, the fun deflated from our game like air from a balloon, and decided to pack it in and retreat home for something more entertaining. Whatever they had given Kevin at the place we called the funny farm had worked this time and was definitely going to have broad market appeal. If I had known about Pfizer at the time, I would have been buying some stock!

CHAPTER 8

The More the Merrier

Dubuque, Iowa was a town of about 55,000 residents, and it had a decidedly Catholic personality. Back in the sixties and seventies, there were an abundance of Catholic churches and bars. The town voters even once elected a Catholic nun, Sister Carolyn Farrell, as Mayor. On Sunday mornings, no matter what part of town we were in, we could hear church bells ringing from about six a.m. until noon, when the last service was completed. Lore has it that the reason there were so many churches and bars was because the majority of the population's ancestors had immigrated from Catholic backgrounds in Germany and Ireland, and despite the Catholic heritage they shared, they could not bring themselves to integrate their ethnic differences when praying or drinking. Eventually, however, there were mixed marriages of Irish and German Catholics, and the melting pot began—a true example of diversity at its finest.

One of the teachings within the Catholic faith is that marriage is, in large part, about procreation; therefore, the Church endorsed no artificial means of birth control. The priests all openly discouraged the use of condoms, foams, gels, IUDs, and the God-forbidden 'pill' during their remarks from the pulpit. As a result, there were many large families around town. Having six to eight children in a family was quite common, and it was not unheard of to have twelve or fourteen. My friend Troy Budde was twelfth in a family of fifteen. We traditionally think of nieces or nephews being born to living aunts and uncles, but in Uncle Troy's case, he already had several nieces and nephews when he was born, and one of his nieces even babysat him when he was a young boy.

One of the great things about so many large families was the number of kids to play with around the neighborhood. We had three different neighborhood baseball teams, each consisting of about twelve players, all from a six-square-block area. Each teams roster included a number of brothers. Had the lineups been announced over a P.A. system before games, it would have gone something like: Batting leadoff, and playing second base, Neuhaus. In the two slot, and playing left field, Neuhaus. The third hitter, playing first base, Neuhaus, and so on.

From the time school let out around June 1 until classes resumed the last week of August, we played baseball, baseball, and more baseball. We played against our neighborhood teams, against other teams in the city recreation league, and against anyone who was available; regardless of whom they were, in the evenings on the field near the junior high school. Typically, the day ended at the baseball field around nine fifteen or nine thirty p.m., when someone got hit with a line drive that they could not see coming due to the night darkness. That would be the game ender.

Many a summer night, after baseball was through, fifteen or more kids from the neighborhood would congregate at 116 to engage in a variety of group games: flashlight tag, kick the can, Red Rover, and others. Sometimes we would all just sit on the big limestone wall in front of the house or lie in the moist evening grass and tell ghost stories. After the incident I had with Greg, I did more listening than telling.

When the heat and humidity set in during the July and August afternoons, it became uncomfortably sticky. These conditions made it virtually unbearable to play more than just a few hours of baseball. On the most humid of days, we ventured to the local Holiday

Inn about six blocks from 116 and helped ourselves to the pool that was intended for the guests. All of us would memorize a fake room number so we would be prepared when a hotel staff member became suspicious and inquired as to our last name and what room we were staying in. We would respond quickly with "Jones, Room 212" or "Smith, Room 321." When the staffer walked back to the front desk to attempt to validate our claim, we ran like hell across the hot asphalt parking lot in our bare feet in a desperate move to evade being busted and having our parents called to come and get us. We usually got away with this about twice per week for a couple of weeks before our faces became too familiar and lodged us on the radar of all employees. We had to chill out for a few weeks before resuming the game. It seemed the thrill of having to be prepared to escape without incident became equally as much fun as splashing about in the cool water to escape the dreadful heat of summer.

In 1965, if one were to stand in the middle of Nevada Street on a summer day, looking north up the street, they would witness endless rows of mature Elm trees that lined the street on both sides, their arched branches and many leaves creating a natural tunnel that shaded the entire street like a covered bridge. By 1970, the scene had changed dramatically and permanently as the result of a fungus that became known as Dutch Elm disease. The disease, caused by feeding on the roots of the Elms by some species of bark beetle caused the rapid decline of most all the Elms that lined many streets in the neighborhood. One of the things I remember most vividly about summers in the late 1960's were the hordes of kids from up and down the street gathering on the Nevada Street terrace at 116 to sit and watch the City of Dubuque Street and Parks crews work endlessly at the removal of the dead and dying trees. It was a fascinating process to watch, and we would often settle in to our viewing area around eight in the morning and not lose interest until perhaps the workers broke for lunch.

The way it worked was that a few big army-green city dump trucks arrived in the morning, one of them pulling a huge gasoline-operated wood-chipping machine on wheels behind it. There would be a crew of six or seven men, each with his specific role to play in the process. Typically, two guys, wearing hard hats and spiked boots, with chainsaws anchored to their big leather tool belts, would scale to the top of a tree that had been marked for demolition a few days earlier by a separate crew that had come by with red spray paint and marked an X on the trunk of the trees that had received the death sentence. When the two climbers reached the top, they pulled out their chainsaws and started clipping off limbs that would fall thirty or forty feet from the sky before smashing into and shattering on the asphalt street. After the climbers had shaved off five or six limbs, they took a break, steadying themselves against the trunk of the tree with their spiked boots dug into the bark and their leather tool belts serving as a harness, wrapped around them and the tree. At this point, two or three men below walked into the street and started dragging the spent branches to the chipper, where two others guided them into the machine that would grind them up, making a loud buzzing noise as it gobbled them to mulch and spit them in very small pieces, right into the back of the dump truck. The process was repeated as the climbers worked their way down the tree, taking every limb off until they reached the bottom. When the limbs were all removed, one climber went back up with his chainsaw and started buzzing through three-to four-foot sections of the tree trunk, letting them tumble to the street for chipping. When the climber got down to a part of the tree where the trunk was too thick for him, he climbed down, and several saws worked at cutting a wedge out of the base of the trunk until the remaining part of the tree tipped over, making a thunderous and Earth-shaking *BOOM* as it hit the street. After the tree was entirely removed and chipped, the last order of business was to pull out a few push brooms and clean sweep the street of lingering remnants. The entire process usually took about three hours. Another crew always came by a few days later and removed the stump, then filled the cavity that was left behind with some dirt and a little grass seed.

This went on for the better part of two summers until there was hardly a tree left for as far as we could see. A few people who lived on Nevada planted new trees, and over the course of five or six years, these helped to make the memory of the tragic loss of the great Elms less unsettling. Still, the street as we knew it had changed forever.

Another occurrence that seemed to bring every summer kid from within twelve square blocks of 116 out of the woodwork was the annual dump truck load of sand Mom had delivered around the first week of June, after school let out. Like clockwork, around June 4 or 5, a big green and white dump truck from Dubuque Sand & Gravel backed up in the alley behind 116 and dropped about two tons of sand in one big pile on the edge of our backyard where it bordered the alley. Within hours, word would spread near and far that the sand had arrived, and about twenty kids between the ages of six and twelve would have already dug into the pile and gotten busy creating a variety of interesting uses for the good stuff. First, there would be a King of the Hill battle until the sand began to tumble down and spread out, creating a twenty-foot square, borderless, two-foot deep sandbox. Kids dug tunnels, built forts and castles, and buried themselves and others entirely from their toes to their chins, leaving only heads exposed. Sometimes it would be hard to even identify who you were looking at under all of the sand. There were toy cars and trucks, plastic action figures, shovels, buckets, and dozens of those little green plastic miniature army men. We built little cities and used houses and hotels from our Monopoly games for effect. My brother Ken even got the idea one day to build a scale model of Wrigley Field out of sand, grass, cardboard, and a few other improvised items. We thought it looked pretty authentic. Smoke bombs, sparklers, and firecrackers became some of the more popular props used to enhance the gritty fun. Standard procedure after playing for hours in the sand was to stand with legs spread wide apart and arms spread out while someone else sprayed you off with the garden hose. It was the best way to do an initial cleaning before heading home for a shower or bath. For about eight dollars, which is what the whole truckload of sand cost, lots of people had endless hours of good and creative fun, and Mom could keep an eye on most of the neighborhood with just an occasional glance out her back porch window.

CHAPTER 9

Search for Tomorrow

Another favorite summer activity was one we called 'Search for Tomorrow', which became a code phrase we would use to communicate with one another about sneaking into our best friends' house while they were away so we could steal their snack foods.

The Schute family lived on our block, and they were arguably our best friends—the guys we spent the most time with. Mike was my brother Tom's age, and Mike's brother, who was also named Tom, was a year older than me. We also shared some mutual cousins with the Schutes, so we presumed that made us family, and we referred to one another simply as 'Cuz'. The four of us could actually have passed for being from the same family, and we were often confused by adults in the neighborhood as being related. It was handy for all of us because when an adult felt the need to report one of our misdeeds to our parents (like urinating outside), we could easily claim a case of mistaken identity with the Schute's; likewise, the Schute's would claim the same with their parents. It worked pretty well for a long while, and we usually got away with it.

We applied this theory in our approach to the multiple daily trips we made back and forth from 116 to the Schutes' house. Rather than walking halfway around the block, we hopped over the three wire mesh fences that enclosed the three private yards that separated 116 from the Schutes' residence. We ran toward the first fence, grabbed one of the metal poles that held it up, and swung around the pole, landing on the other side of the fence. We then repeated the action two more times until we were at the Schutes' back door. We thought it was efficient, though the people who owned and maintained the fences somehow thought otherwise.

Search for Tomorrow was actually the name of a soap opera our three older sisters watched on summer afternoons when they did not have a babysitting gig. The way this code came into being is something we should have been ashamed of and filled with Catholic guilt over, but I guess we simply had no morals when it came to snack food. On Mary's many trips to the Warehouse Market, one thing she rarely—if ever—returned home with was snack food of any kind. It was not that she was concerned for our health as much as the fact that snack food cost too much, and there was no room in the grocery budget for such luxuries. The Schutes however, had only five kids and perhaps slightly more income than the Neuhaus family. Mrs. Schute had a whole drawer in the kitchen filled with candy, cookies, bubble gum, and other treats. It was referred to in appropriately simple fashion as 'the snack drawer'. They also bought all of the best kinds of sugared cereals of the day: Cap'n Crunch, Apple Jacks, Honeycomb, Fruit Loops, Count Chocula, and others. The Neuhaus cereal cabinet had Cheerios, Rice Krispies, and Corn Flakes. Yuck! There wasn't an ounce of sugar in any of them.

One summer afternoon, Tom Schute and I were sitting on the couch on their screened-in porch, where we often sat on summer afternoons when a break was in order. Mrs. Schute had given us a bottle of Hires Root Beer to split. She poured equal amounts in each of our cups. As I was about to drink mine, Tom stopped me and asserted that if we poured the caramel-colored soda from cup to cup and mixed them up, it would make more root beer. I was no chemist and was all in favor of more root beer, so I gave him my cup, and he began to pour the contents from one into the other and repeated the exercise several times. He then held his cup forward and showed me the contents. Sure enough, there was more Hires in his cup. It had worked! We could make more root beer anytime we wanted. It made sense because of the Bible story we had heard at Nativity Church and School about Jesus making plenty more wine, bread, and fish from a meager amount at the wedding celebration—enough to entertain the masses. This was awesome! Tom began to drink from his cup, but when I reached for my cup and lifted it to my salivating kisser, it became obvious all he had done was pour some of mine into his. When I contested this, he put the cups together and showed how they were equal. The issue, of course, was that he had already taken a big swig from his.

Mrs. Schute interrupted at this point when she walked out on the porch to tell Tom it was time to take him and his younger siblings to their dentist appointments. The house was going to be empty for at least two hours. There were more Hires on the landing of the stairs that led to their basement, and I felt I deserved compensation for Tom's little miracle. I asked Mrs. Schute if I could use the bathroom before I left. "Of course," she said.

The bathroom on the main level of the house was off the kitchen, which we entered from the porch. I walked from the porch to the kitchen, hung a quick right, and was into the bathroom, which conveniently had a window to the screen porch, which I proceeded to unlock. I flushed the toilet to create the impression it had been used, and then I bid the Schutes farewell. Tom agreed to call me when he got home from the dentist so we could hang out some more. I watched from behind the hedges as the turquoise-colored Mercury Comet exited the drive and headed down Langworthy Avenue. Off to the dentist they went, and in through the bathroom window went I, on a quest for root beer revenge! I got a full bottle of Hires and began to suck it down. As I sat at the kitchen table where Mrs. Schute was often so kind as to feed us lunch in the summer, the snack drawer came in to larger-than-life focus. My conscience and Bible lessons aside, I couldn't help myself. *Snack on, Rogey!* I pulled open the drawer with great visions of all that was likely in there, and I was not disappointed. I grabbed two Almond Joy bars and a Snirkel, which was a caramel block bar with white marshmallow filling swirled in its center. Out the main door of the house I went, making sure to lock it behind me.

I was feeling both a bit guilty, but also somewhat exuberant, at my sneaky score as I unassumingly took the unusual path around the block back to 116. I did not want anyone to see me bolting across the fences and yards from the scene of the candy caper, snack gone wrong heist. When I got home, my brother Tom was there, talking about walking down to Frank and John's Gulf Station to buy some candy. I decided I had to let him in on the secret. I whispered to him, "I know where we can get it for free" in a subtle tone so our sisters, who were watching <u>Search for Tomorrow</u>, would not hear me. We headed for the Schute's house, right back in the open bathroom window and back to the snack drawer. Tom suggested we had time for a couple of bowls of Cap'n Crunch as well, as long as we washed the bowls and put them away when we were done. It seemed like a good idea at the time.

From that day forward, the code was used to communicate with one another the fact that no one was home at the Schute house and it was time to search for snacks. We even got as bold as to ask probing questions of various family members as to their schedules for the day so we could figure the best time to conduct the Search for Tomorrow. The Schutes were our best friends after all, so what harm could there be in assuming they would want to share the wealth?

The lesson learned here should have been the Eleventh Commandment: Though shalt not covet thy neighbor's snacks.

CHAPTER 10

Mark Mac

While the Schute boys were particularly close when it came to our inner circle, we had a myriad of neighbors and buddies from school we spent a lot of time with, and they were a fascinating crew. Among those in the neighborhood was Mark McLaughlin, our next-door neighbor. Mark was the lone boy in his family, which included three sisters. The Neuhaus brothers, by virtue of mere proximity, became his surrogate brothers. Mark was the only left-handed kid on the block; so naturally, he was a pitcher and first baseman on our neighborhood team, the Nevada Sluggers. Mark and his father, Bob, were huge St. Louis Cardinals fans, and Mark wore the red cap with the interwoven cursive white letters S and L embroidered above the bill of the cap to prove it. This was a stark contrast to the Neuhaus family, all of who had lost their Major League Baseball virginity at Wrigley Field in Chicago and were stalwart Cubs fans. The rivalry was playful, yet with an occasional edge, particularly when the two teams competed in televised weekend series, and we would begin to wager our hard-earned paper route money on the outcome of the games.

One of the things I really appreciated about 'Mark Mac', as we called him, was his sympathy for a bit of a podiatric condition I had as a young boy that required that I wear special corrective shoes. Between the ages of about five and ten, I absolutely despised trips to the shoe store. My mom took my brothers and me for new shoes before the start of each school year. Ken, Tom, and Greg always got to pick out what they wanted from whatever shoes were in style that year: PF Flyers, Hush Puppies, Converse Chuck Taylor edition, or whatever. For me, it was always the hard, plain ugly black corrective shoes from Fred Pape at the Fred Pape Shoe Store, who would lace me up with the ugly dorky dogs year in and year out. The only thing that ever changed was the size Fred would prescribe. It left me feeling quite like Charlie Brown must have felt when he went trick or treating on the night of the Great Pumpkin. Charlie got a rock; I got Fred Pape black shoes. Good grief!

Knowing the awkwardness and sheer agony the black shoes caused for me, Mark Mac oftentimes brought an extra pair of his much cooler shoes for me to borrow when we were playing away from the neighborhood and there was no risk of my parents finding out. I hid the ghastly black boats in the bushes, slipped on Mark's extra pair, and made the re-change before going home. I was grateful for Mark's kind gesture that gave me so much temporary freedom and relief.

Although Mark may have been slightly disappointed about being stuck in a house with three sisters, his misfortune was seen—in the most literal sense of the word—as a wonderful windfall by the boys next door. As mentioned earlier, 116 sat immediately next to the McLaughlins' house. The small grassy area that separated them spanned only about twenty feet, so they were quite close together on one side. The construct of both houses was similar in that the living and dining areas were on the main floor, and each had three bedrooms upstairs. As fate would have it, the bedroom I shared with my three brothers for part of the time we were growing up had a direct view, at the same level, as a bedroom shared by two of Mark's sisters. By circumstances that were at least partly calculated (and sometimes just serendipitous), my brothers and I would end up in our bedroom some steamy summer nights with our lights turned out, right about the time the McLaughlin girls' bedroom light would come on. Into the room they would saunter to prepare for sleep. Crouched to the floor, battling for position at the base of our window, we would quietly and nervously peer across the way on the dark summer eve to see the girls wiggle out of their shorts and fling off their halter tops as they slipped into sleek, semi-transparent baby-doll nightwear. We cherished every illicit moment, as they stood in front of the mirror in their hip-length nighties, stroking their hair with a brush until the kinks caused by the humidity of the day had been smoothed out. It was truly, the things pre-adolescent dreams were made of. We were thankful the McLaughlin's did not have all boys. Besides having a good friend in Mark, it was yet another reason to appreciate the McLaughlins living so close.

CHAPTER 11

Phelper

Unlike the McLaughlin's, the Pierotti family, just half a block up and across Nevada Street, had three boys: Steve, Doug, and Dave. Their father was the athletic director at the Catholic high school in town, so they were all sports minded and dreamed of winning scholarships to Notre Dame. Since they were then just twelve, ten, and nine years old, however, they settled for hosting the weekly Sunday-afternoon neighborhood 'tackle the man with the ball' game in their long, rectangular, well-manicured yard. Typically, an autumn Sunday afternoon would find about ten or twelve of us on the Pierotti lawn playing this basic game that only young boys behaving like a large litter of puppies could love. It worked like this: We took one of those foam-rubber Nerf footballs and tossed it straight up in the air. As it came down, the whole pack leaped skyward, arms extended vertically, attempting to pull down the ball. Whoever hauled it in took off running, followed by the thundering herd, whose shared sole objective became to catch, tackle, and pile atop the ball carrier while wrestling the sponge ball from his grasp, to win the prize of becoming the next man pursued by the roving band. As a result of this beloved activity, every pair of Levi's and

Wrangler jeans we owned became grass stained, and none of us possessed a sweatshirt or football jersey that didn't have a torn collar. Needless to say, this was not a popular activity with the moms on the block or anyone else who was responsible for laundering and sewing in their respective households.

Mr. Welp lived next door to the Pierottis. He worked as a delivery truck driver for a local dairy. The taxi-yellow mobile he drove had the cab of a large pick-up truck, but mounted on the back was an oversized refrigerated box that encased and preserved the dairy products he routed to grocery stores and restaurants. 'Phelper', as we nicknamed him without his knowledge, parked the truck in an alley behind his garage each night when he returned from his route. Inside the wooden chocolate brown garage were three white commercial-sized freezers with big lids on top, which were mounted to hinges and had handles to swing them upward to open. From observing Phelper's comings and goings, loading and unloading his truck, it was hard for young boys not to notice there appeared to be some rather enticing cargo being transferred. We agreed this required further investigation.

One brisk November evening, when the trees no longer wore leaves but the aroma of them burning in the night air carried on until the yards in the neighborhood were free of them, we set out to investigate. The mission presented three primary obstacles. First, we needed to get into the garage, which had a swinging door like that of a horse stable, but was fastened shut with a shiny silver metal bracket and key-access padlock. Second, we needed to navigate around the garage to find the freezers without turning on any lights. Finally, when we got to the freezers, we needed to figure out the contents of each one, in large part utilizing mostly just the sense of touch, because any light we might use to aid the exploration posed a risk of being seen through the garage window from the kitchen window in Phelper's house, about twenty yards from the garage.

After a good deal of scheming and what we believed to be think tank activity of the highest order, we arrived at a plan. Three of us would slowly and casually walk down the alley, bypassing the truck and garage and scoping out all we could in terms of the best approach for trying to gain entry to the garage. We figured traveling *en masse* would make it appear as though we were just walking home or some other unassuming place. As we wandered by the garage and fixated on the padlock, we could not believe our eyes. Phelper had hung the lock through the silver metal bracket, but had failed to snap the bar on the lock into the hole it needed to be inserted in to *click* and take hold. The garage was not locked, and we would not have to go to the trouble of using the screwdriver to remove the screws that held the bracket in place. Yes! We regrouped in the Pierotti's yard and began to discuss the next steps: Who would enter the garage? Who would stand look out? How would the rest of us signal any imminent danger to the intruder, should Phelper come out or a car comes down the alley? And so on. After more plotting, we all accepted various roles, and the caper was on. Dave, the youngest and most daring of the Pierotti boys, volunteered to be the single man to enter the garage. The code we would shout aloud to warn him to abort the mission if something went wrong was "Ollie Ollie oxen free!" a term we would commonly shout out in the neighborhood to signal the end of a game of hide and seek when the seeker wanted to tell the remaining hiders that he had given up on finding them and was ready to concede the game. There would be nothing unusual about one of us yelling that phrase, and we knew it should draw no suspicion.

Dave disappeared into the Pierotti's house for a short while and returned wearing a black hooded sweatshirt (torn around the collar), black sweat pants, and a black stocking cap. Like something from a scene out of a crime thriller movie, his brother Doug, shifting into makeup artist mode, proceeded to color Dave's cheeks black with a piece of charcoal. If this mission were to fail, it would most certainly not be due to a lack of foresight. We had the bases covered, and it was time to execute.

Rather than walking down the alley, this time Dave crawled on all fours down the grassy bank from Pierotti's house to the fence that enclosed Phelper's yard, then dropped on his chest to the ground and proceeded to belly crawl the length of the outside of the chain-link fence to the door of the garage. He arose to a crouch when he reached the door and then easily slipped the lock out of the bracket. He propped the door open just wide enough to allow entry by his thin frame, and then it closed. Dave was in! Those of us on lookout slapped a quiet, restrained, yet celebratory high-five, knowing what we believed would be the greatest obstacle at the outset of our planning had been overcome.

We were all thinking about what kind of contraband Dave would come back with for us when suddenly and without warning, the floodlight that had the ability to illuminate Phelper's whole backyard came on and lit things up like a baseball stadium. Heart rates increased, and frantic and scrambled thoughts now ruled. We had arrived at a crisis point, but "Ollie, Ollie oxen free" no longer appeared the failsafe we had concocted it to be. We were all expecting Phelper to step out the back door of the house at any moment, but it didn't happen. To our relief, the floodlight was on a timer, and there was no one there.

Relieved for the moment, but experiencing a heightened sense of vulnerability, we suspected Dave needed to get out short of what we had hoped for in terms of the take. But we forgot one important thing: Dave had no fear. There was a reason he was the one in the garage.

As we watched for signs of activity in and outside the garage from our safe, distant, perch, the big brown garage door began to creak. It was Dave, exiting and placing the lock back in place. He disappeared down the alley, into the night, unable to return the way he had approached the garage because of the bright beams cast by the floodlight. Minutes later, Dave came around the corner of the Pierotti's house and into the yard where we had surveyed the operation. He was laughing like a madman and jumping up and down, dropping box after box of the good stuff from under his sweatshirt and out of the hood he had filled as well. There were ice cream bars, Scooter Crunch bars, Bomb Pops, and Fudgesicles. He had grabbed four boxes with six items per box.

We feasted on frozen delights until our bellies were ready to burst. It didn't matter that we were outside on the kind of night that could easily have brought the first snowfall of the season. The heat generated in a great and victorious battle warmed us. "This must be like the feeling of running a touchdown into the end zone in front of Touchdown Jesus in South Bend," Dave remarked.

I could only think this was not something I would want Jesus to know anything about.

CHAPTER 12

The Lyness Brothers

The Lyness brothers, Steve and John, lived just one block up Solon Street and two doors to the right at Alpine street . . . well; they didn't really *live* there. Their Grandma Coleman lived at 89 Alpine. It was more a place they would appear at for a period of time and vanish from without much warning. Back in those days, it seemed no parents ever divorced. In fact, Steve and John were the only guys we actually knew who were the product of a broken home. When we first met them around the ages of five and six, their last name was Conrad. Shortly thereafter, their dad bolted. We had never met him, but we had seen photos of him in his U.S. Army uniform in Vietnam. After he left, they started going by the last name Coleman, their mother's maiden name. Then, their mom married a guy named George Lyness, and once again, the boys had a new last name. Though I never verbalized it, I was always disturbed by the thought that something as personal as a boy's name could change just like that on the whims of another person. It was so foreign of a concept to me. I could not imagine having more than one last name. It seemed like such an assault to a person's very identity and the sense of heritage and stability that is supposed to come with it. It also struck me very odd that someone's father could simply disappear, and some other guy with a different name could show up and just take his place. I felt bad for the boys. It seemed they had been cheated out of what should have been one of the most basic things in life: the two people who brought them into the world and the name they were given at that time. While the brothers didn't ever complain about their personal family life, it was obvious they were missing something all the rest of the kids in the neighborhood had. Not long after their mom married George, they packed up and moved to Dallas, Texas. At that point, they were the only people we knew who had moved out of Dubuque. It was sad to see them go, but we soon learned they would not be gone forever.

George, which is what they always called him (not 'Dad') and their mom had a child of their own the first year they were in Texas. When school got out for the summer, Steve and John reappeared at 89 Alpine to live with Grandma Coleman for the summer giving their mom and George time to become a new family with their baby sister back in Texas. This ended up becoming the routine for the next five or six summers. We were always excited when the Texas boys—who had developed a strange Texas way of speaking—showed up at our door around the first week of June. They would be a part of everything we did for the following ten weeks. They loved it, and so did we. I suspect summers at Grandma Coleman's were probably the fondest memories of their childhood.

We had a lot of fun with the Lyness boys. As you might assume, living with Grandma Coleman required little discipline. There were no real rules and no chores to be done. She let them come and go as they pleased, and she even bought them matching bright yellow ten-speed bicycles to get around. There was no set time for them to be home for meals. It was pretty much a free-for-all. All of us who lived with real parents were envious. Another bonus to living with Grandma Coleman was that she was gone from her house often. She attended church, dinner parties, card games, and more. Once in a while, she even left town for a few days, and the boys had the house pretty much to themselves, except for the occasional visit from their uncle, Bill Morehouse, who would stop by sporadically to check on them.

The saying "when the cat is away, the mice will play" could not have been any more analogous to the situation of Grandma Coleman leaving town, and the Lyness boys being home alone. The only thing was, they were never really completely alone. When word got out that their grandmother was away, about ten of us would converge on 89 Alpine and take the place over as our very own pad. As we got to be twelve, thirteen, and fourteen years old, there were always a couple of us who were able to convince our older brothers to buy us a few twelve-packs of beer and a box of Swisher Sweets cigars. We slid the extension into Grandma's dining room table, broke out her playing cards and poker chips, drank beer, smoked cigars, and played poker with our paper route money until we all passed out or someone got sick. As far as we knew, we thought we had the world by the tail.

Another piece of mischief that was a standard when Grandma was away involved getting into the bottle of Jim Beam whiskey she kept in the pantry. We sipped it straight or mixed it with Coke and then refilled the bottle to about the level it had been at by adding a few ounces of water. One afternoon, when she was out of town, we had been sipping on the Jim Beam pretty good when Uncle Bill walked through the door for one of his drop-in visits to check up on his nephews.

Bill was a pretty cool guy, but he was the one person in Steve and John's summer lives who was known to throw down a little discipline once in a while. On this afternoon, Bill was pretty excited. He played in an over-thirty softball league and had a game to go to that evening. When he came upon us, he had just come from Zehtener's Sporting Goods Store, where he had purchased a new softball glove. As new gloves always are, his was quite stiff and needed some breaking in to make it more flexible before the night's game. "Hey, guys, let's play some catch," he said.

Unbeknownst to him, we were all a bit too tipsy for that, but he was insistent, so we wound up in the front yard at 89 Alpine trying to play catch with Uncle Bill to help him break in his new glove.

The exercise started out with my brother Tom, Steve Lyness, and Bill playing three-way. When the ball came to Tom or Steve, it was all they could do to catch it. Then, about every other time they tossed it to Bill, it was either at his feet in the grass or over his head, and he ended up having to chase it down the big hill in the neighbor's yard behind him. During one of Bill's adventures to track down an errant throw, Steve and Tom told John and me to take over. Bad went to worse, with Bill getting hit in the shins on bad bounces and huffing and puffing after throws over his head to the point where he surrendered and called the game off. Knowing that we all lived and died baseball in the summers, Bill asked, "What is wrong with you guys? I know you're much better than this." He had seen us play many times before, and he was right. We started making excuses that he did not buy, and then he came over and smelled Steve's breath. "Have you boys been drinking?" Bill inquired suspiciously. Steve caved in and said he had drunk one of his grandma's Potosi beers because he was thirsty and there was no soda in the house. After that, Bill told Tom and me it was time to head home, and he locked up the house and took Steve and John over to his place. We were cold busted and unfortunately, too sober to ignore it.

CHAPTER 13

Take Me to the River . . . and Back

We rode our bikes all over Dubuque in the summer when we were kids. Our parents rarely knew exactly where we were, but they usually had at least some notion of who we were with and probably an idea of three or four places they might find us if they looked. These were the days before missing children's photos ever appeared on the side of milk cartons, so the basic rules were to be home in time to deliver your papers at three thirty, be home again at six for dinner (with all family members seated at the table together), and then be home when the streetlights come on. In the summertime in Dubuque, that was around nine thirty p.m., but who really knew?

A favorite place we used to ride was down Third Street, which was about a half-mile long. A small portion of it was a hill that started up above the tree-lined bluffs of the city, and at the bottom poured bikers out onto the flat downtown area that led to the banks of the Mississippi River. Some of the guys had speedometers on their bikes, so the challenge, of course, was to see how far we could push the red needle as we sailed down Third Street with the wind whistling in our ears. The fastest I recall us topping out at was about forty MPH. Lance Armstrong would have been proud. When we got down to the river, a lot of our time would be occupied by throwing small tree branches in to the muddy current and then bombing it with rocks, trying to crack it into pieces before it could escape south toward the Julien Dubuque Bridge.

The Illinois Central Railroad had tracks that crossed the river over a rickety wooden bridge that was portable in that a large portion of the center part of the bridge, which was operated from a little control shack out in the middle, opened, rotating at a 180° angle so that barges carrying coal, grain, and corn up and down the river could pass without their tops hitting the base of the bridge. It was a strange scene to look down the tracks from the west side of the bridge and see the center open. If a train did come at that time, it would roll right off the bridge, car after car, down into the water.

We walked out onto the bridge for thrills. It was about three quarters of a mile across from Iowa to Illinois, though we would never risk walking all the way across. I mean really, what would you do if the portable part swung open while you were on that section? It was too much to risk, even for us former ice cream and candy thieves. We could look down between the tracks and see the river rushing by about fifty feet below. It was a pretty sobering feeling to be far enough out on the bridge to the point where we knew that if suddenly that dreaded single headlight appeared from the darkness of the cave trains came out of from the East Dubuque, Illinois side, we would be challenged to either jump into the river or out run the train back to the Dubuque, Iowa side of the bridge. We might have been able to stand far off to the edge of the track while the train passed within a foot or so of your face, but that seemed like a poor third option. We had a few close calls, but never had to take the leap into the river.

Another amusing thing we did to pass time down on the tracks was to set coins on the rail and wait for a train to come and run over them. Oftentimes, the vibration of the rail or the wind the boxcars created as they rhythmically swayed by us swept the coins away, never to be reclaimed. The first time I actually saw what the train did to a penny, however, made quite an impression (pardon the pun). It was flattened to about ten percent of its original thickness, and expanded to about three times its original diameter. It was as smooth as glass; all printing and indentations on the coin were gone, including any signs of Abe Lincoln's face on the front or the Lincoln memorial on the back or the year it was minted. That was probably the day the concept of recycling truly registered with me when I saw firsthand how something could be returned to its original, most basic elements.

After the Illinois Central tracks crossed the river on to Iowa soil, they rolled about two hundred yards past the Dubuque Star Brewery, Iowa's first home to beer-making, and the Shot Tower, a tall rock structure in which pellets for muskets were produced during the Civil War, then the tracks bent gradually around the silver sheet metal center and left field fences of Johnny Petrakis Park. 'Petrakis', as we called it, was the consummate Minor League Class A baseball stadium of the 1960s and 1970s—the type that could be found in a dozen towns in Iowa, Illinois, and Wisconsin. Together, they comprised the playing locations for the Midwest league. If you have seen the film <u>Bull Durham</u>, it was just like the place the Durham Bulls played. There was even a real-life legend by the name of Moe Hill who played for Wisconsin Rapids, the Minnesota Twins affiliate, who mirrored the Crash character Kevin Costner played in the classic film. Many a summer eve, we hung out on the tracks, heckling the opposing teams' left fielder, throwing rocks at the metal fence, and occasionally letting one soar over onto the field and near the player. We always considered it a high honor when the opposing fielder complained to the umpire and the man in blue walked out toward us from second base with a threatening gesture, as though we would be expelled somehow from the tracks if the behavior did not cease. When the home team, the Dubuque Packers, came out to play, we cheered and bowed to our left fielder in attempts to get him to acknowledge our presence on the track. The few times we got a tip of the cap usually resulted after the opponent had just complained to the umpire in the bottom half of the previous inning. It was our guy's way of saying, "Keep up the harassment." They appeared to really get a kick out of it.

Dubuque is a hilly town—and not just some slight inclines. I'm talking absolutely super-steep hills, particularly from the downtown up the bluffs to the plateau that is the rest of the city. One exceptionally exhausting humid afternoon, after we had finished playing down by the river and really did not feel like pumping our bicycle pedals up the monster incline home, we found ourselves at the base of Fourth Street and the downtown end of the tracks and pulley that constitute the Fourth Street elevator, the cable car.

The Fourth Street elevator is a unique pulley-and-cable-guided form of rail transport. Two small-enclosed carts that can seat about six people each are guided up and down the steepest of bluffs for about one quarter of a mile. One car begins at the bottom downtown, and the other begins at the top of the elevator on the edge of the Dubuque plateau. When the rider at the bottom tugs on a twine cord to signal the operator in the house at the top that they are ready to roll, a return signal—a double buzz—confirms receipt of the message, and with a sudden jerk, the thin-walled wooden car begins its ascent up the side of the steep hill. Halfway up the hill, the track divides into two sections so the upward and downward carts can pass one another without colliding. After passing on the separate sections of track, they proceed in their set directions, occupying the track previously traveled by the car that is going the opposite direction. The entire ride only lasts about two minutes, but the ease it provides compared to the alternative for climbing the hill is truly remarkable. Near the dawn of the twentieth century, a local well-to-do businessman constructed the elevator as his personal means for getting from his downtown office to his home atop the bluff. It allowed him the ability to go home for lunch each day and made the otherwise tough terrain easily navigable. After a period of time, he recognized the commercial value and began to charge others a fare to utilize his invention. By the time I was a kid, the elevator had become more a novelty—a tourist excursion experience and a source of local historical preservation pride.

As we pried the doors of the cable car gently apart so we could enter, with our bikes taken in and leaned against one side of the passenger car, we wondered how the operator at the top would respond to the transporting of the bikes. We had never attempted this before. When we reached the top and escorted our ten-speeds out of the car and toward the turn-style, where our ten-cent fare was due, the operator looked at us with a raised eyebrow and a befuddled look. "That'll be ten cents for each of you boys . . . and I guess ten cents for each of the bikes."

We settled up at twenty cents each, which we deemed well worth it. And thus, a trend was created. Within two weeks, the fare sign at the operators' gate that originally read 10 cents each way, 15 cents round-trip had a line added to it at the bottom that read Bicycles 10 cents each way.

CHAPTER 14

Catfish Creek and Twin Sisters

While trips down to the river were a standard among our summertime adventures, we also had a few other regular spots that were high on our list for outdoor amusement. Among them was a tributary of the Mississippi River known as Catfish Creek. Catfish Creek twisted and turned, pretty much following a railroad track, from its origin somewhere unknown to us out toward the west end of Dubuque. What we did know well of Catfish, however, began at the point where a small bridge crossed over it down in a valley, as we descended the steep hill that was Fremont Avenue, near Wartburg Seminary. This access to Catfish was about a two-mile walk from 116, but once we reached the bridge at the bottom of Fremont and turned left onto the railroad tracks, what had been city quickly became a rural wonderland that could occupy the better part of a day.

Whenever we went to Catfish Creek, it was automatic that we would take our BB guns. As we wandered down the tracks that shadowed the creek, we fired at virtually anything that moved in the tall weeds and woods along the way. About a mile down the tracks east of where our expedition started at Fremont, we came across a landmark spot where we always wandered off the tracks and up a few hundred yards of dirt path to do some climbing at a place called Twin Sisters. Twin Sisters consisted of two huge rock formations that stood side-by-side, rising about two hundred feet in elevation and separated by only about a four-foot crack between them. We ascended the path to the big rocks until reaching their base, at which time we stacked our guns in nearby brush because from this point on, climbing up the sides of the monsters and negotiating the various crevices and branches that would aide us in our quest would require both feet and both hands if we were to succeed in making it to the top. Reaching the top of Twin Sisters took a combination of guts, patience, and technique. It was something we did more than a few times each season, but it demanded our full efforts every time and really never got any easier.

After becoming satisfied with our climbing experience, we journeyed onward down the tracks another mile or so toward the point where Catfish widens considerably just prior to pouring its waters into the mighty Mississippi. The walk along the tracks could become tiring on a hot summer day, with the strong odor of creosote vapors seeping from the railroad ties all the way along the route. On a good day, we could hitch a ride on a slow-moving freight train and ride it to near the end of the line before it turned and began to pick up speed as the tracks bended south to follow the Mississippi all the way downstream to the little river town of Bellevue.

When the creek blended into the river, we knew we had reached a jumping-off point for our day trip. Standing at the base of a 1,000 foot or higher rock and tree-covered bluff and looking up, we could see the cylinder-shaped limestone monument high above us that marked the burial site of the French explorer Julien Dubuque, who had settled the area more than 100 years prior and for whom the town was named. Our next feat was to navigate the twists and turns of the steep and shabbily maintained dirt paths up the bluff and the occasional rock areas that had to be scaled, much like we had done earlier back at Twin Sisters. The journey up the side of the bluff to Julien Dubuque's grave put a good deal of fear into most of us, though we would never admit it. Any slip along the way could have dire consequences, as a fall backward could result in the kind of tragedy we would not allow ourselves to consider. I can recall several times, being about two thirds the way up the bluff to the monument, looking back down at the creek and river below, and being overcome with a feeling of being too afraid to continue with the upward climb, but completely unwilling to concede what had been accomplished by retreating all the way back down. More than once, it took encouraging words from someone in our group to keep our collective movement up on task. When we reached the top, there was always a great sense of relief and accomplishment. Every single time, upon completing the climb, I recall telling myself this would be the last time for me, but without fail, a few weeks would pass, and I would find myself in the same ambivalent place, doing yet again what we both loved and feared.

CHAPTER 15

Craig and Bakes

There were a number of other interesting neighborhood guys. John Bakey looked Japanese. Everybody thought he was, and some kids from other neighborhoods called him 'Jap Boy' to tease him. The reality was that his father, Dick, a state trooper who always had his red-light-equipped cruiser parked in the driveway, had been a veteran of the Korean War. He met John's South Korean mother, during his tour of duty. 'Bakes', as we called him, was a chubby sort of kid, but strong. He would hit the beejeezus out of a baseball and then trot the bases slowly, taunting the opponents by exaggerating the slant of his eyes, pushing them up further as he rounded the bags. It was hysterical to watch, as if he was saying, "Yeah, Jap Boy just kicked your ass . . . and he liked it." Bakes was an expert at two things: revenge and self-deprecating humor.

Craig DeMoss was a little older than most of the kids he hung round with in the neighborhood, but it worked for him and for us because it gave him an entourage of buddies. We all knew somebody who had a car long before any of us could drive. Craig had a 1966 Chevy Impala. It had six taillights: a set of three on the far left and far right ends, just above the rear bumper. When he used the turn signal, the lights on the side indicating the direction he planned to turn lit up in sequence from the inside to the outside, staggered by just a split second, and then repeated the moving sequence until the turn was completed. It was pretty cool for that day and age.

We often found six or eight of us at a time piling into the Impala to head for the Super-20 Drive-In. We liked going to the drive-in for a number of reasons, but the most important was that, unlike the regular theatres or cinemas at the mall, they did not check IDs at the drive-in. I guess they figured if the driver was old enough, the passengers must be, and they didn't want to hold up a line of traffic behind us by requiring I.D. checks on eight people in one car. We were always a little nervous when we approached the admission booth and Craig slipped the car into park; the idle would kick up a notch, right along with our hearts. We each passed our dollar to him ahead of time, and told the booth person how many people were in the car as he reached the corresponding number of bills to them. Just like that, we were in—twelve or thirteen years old, and we were off to see an R-rated movie. Back then, R stood for one thing: bare titties! Imagine the galaxy of hormones firing at once within the confines of the Impala at the Super-20 as we all watched raunchy titles such as Fly-Girls, Teachers Pet, or The Naughty Nurses. This was better than the McLaughlin sisters!

Craig, being a bit older than the rest of us, took a part-time job at age sixteen to help defray some of the expenses associated with owning even an old car. He ran the counter at the local Baskin Robbins, scooping all thirty-one flavors for customers. For us, the best shift he worked was when he was left alone in the store from six until ten p.m. on Sunday evenings and was left responsible for closing the place down for the evening. Let's just say that had the owner ever tried to reconcile the number of ice cream scoops that were served in that four-hour period each Sunday evening with the corresponding cash in the register, an audit surely would have been in order.

CHAPTER 16

Bound for the Big Leagues

The Isenhart brothers lived on the opposite side of Nevada Street, two doors down from 116. Although there were six or eight kids in the house, Chuck and Tom were closest to our age and the ones most a part of our gang. Chuck, or 'Chas', as we would often refer to him, fancied himself a baseball player, though I'm not sure if anyone else would have agreed with him. There was a relief pitcher for the Chicago Cubs back in that day by the name of Ted Abernathy. Abernathy threw with an unorthodox delivery known as 'submarine style', because his arm would rear back and then swing forward from way down below the waist, rising as it came forward, but releasing the ball at an unusually low area somewhere around the hip. All weight would shift from the left side of the body to the right, with the pitcher practically falling off the mound to the right after release. Chas sought to set himself apart from all the rest of us who pitched in the traditional over-the-top style . . . and that he did. Try as he may, he had a lot of difficulty getting the ball over the plate. If batters would be patient and take a lot of pitches, Chas-man was virtually sure to put them on base or give up a towering home run.

One year, when a number of us were playing on the Nativity Parish summer Holy Name League team, Chas started the game as the pitcher. We were playing on a below ground level pit of a field at a local college—the same field where CBS sports personality Greg Gumbel played college ball in the late 60's for Coach Jim Smarjesse and the Loras Duhawks. Because the field sat about 300 feet below street level, there was a high grassy bank, the 'Green Monster of Dubuque' that acted as the left field wall. It was only about 250 feet down the left field line, so most good right-handed hitters that got a hold of one would put it on the grassy bank, and it would be ruled a ground rule double. Because the grassy bank was about 300 feet high and there was a ten-foot high chain-link fence on top of it that actually served as an enclosure to a soccer field up above on the next level, we had never seen anyone hit one out of the yard. In fact, we were certain that no one could. The mightiness of the pokes to the Green Monster tended to be measured by how high they went before disappearing into the deep grass and weeds of the steep bank, and that was it—that is, until Kevin Rhomberg stepped into the batter's box for Holy Trinity against our submarine-style heater, Chas.

In fairness to Chas, Rhomberg was among the best two or three players ever to come out of Dubuque. He was instrumental in helping to win the state championship for Hempstead High School in 1974, and went on to play at the Triple A level with the Milwaukee Brewers and Cleveland Indians, getting called up to the show a few times with each team during September when those kind of players get their chances. I will never forget that historic evening or the moon shots Rhomberg blasted off Chas. In two innings, Chas faced Rhomberg three times. On each of the three occasions, Kevin smacked the ball up and over the Green Monster and over the ten-foot chain-link fence to the soccer field above, each time with room to spare. It was surreal—like something from a Superman or Popeye episode. Either Rhomberg had eaten his spinach or Chas was in need of some kryptonite or something, because it was a display of the most mismatched one-on-one performance of athlete vs. athlete we had ever seen, perhaps even ever known to mankind. After the third towering, effortless shot by Rhomberg, our coach, Shets, stepped to the mound and motioned for my brother Tom to come in from his position in left field to relieve the defeated, deflated Chas-man. As Tom set foot on the mound and Chas dropped the ball into his glove, from my position at first base I heard these sage words of advice muttered to his replacement by Chas: "Keep the ball low. There's no defense behind you." Yes, Chas indeed set himself apart from all other pitchers that memorable night.

CHAPTER 17

Field of Dreams

While we played a lot of baseball on traditional-type fields, there was a unique approach we took one summer to creating a makeshift stadium and adapting the game to fit the venue. One block down Solon Street from 116, to Booth Street, and then one more block left of there, on the corner of Dodge and Booth Streets, sat a public tennis court that was operated by the City of Dubuque Department of Parks and Recreation. The court surface was concrete, with painted yellow boundary lines on it. At the center of the court was a heavy-duty canvas net that stretched across the court and was anchored on each end with sturdy metal poles implanted in the cement that stood about four feet high, just slightly higher than the net. The entire court was surrounded, on its perimeter, by a chain-link fence that rose about fifteen feet above court level. It did an excellent job of keeping errant tennis shots from spilling out onto U.S. 20, the busy highway that locals called Dodge, that bordered it to the south. Also, at the top of the fence, in each of the four corners of the court, were spotlights that allowed for evening play until they turned off automatically around eleven p.m.

One summer night, we were retreating back to 116 after our regular game of baseball on the field at the nearby Washington Junior High School had to be called off due to darkness. None of us were happy that the game had to be called on darkness, because we were deadlocked in a seven-seven tie when Mark McLaughlin bounced a line shot off of Tom Schute's forehead and damn near knocked him out cold. As we were riding our bikes down Dodge Hill, Craig DeMoss commented about the lights being on at the empty tennis court and suggested we finish our stalemate of a game there. As confining as the makeshift baseball surface was, it was lit up like a Christmas tree, so we agreed to make do. Let there be light . . . and there was.

Since the rules needed to be altered to adapt to the space we were in, we decided that any ball hit inside the tennis court that either bounced on the concrete court or rattled off the chain-link fence was an automatic out. The game, in essence, would become a homerun derby. The only way to score was to hit the ball over the fifteen-foot fence for a homerun. We agreed we would only play one more inning, and if no one scored, we would accept a tie. In the top half of the inning, one ball bounced off the net, and the chain-link fence contained two. John Bakey came to the plate in the bottom half of the inning and smacked the first pitch thrown at him clear over the left field fence. We watched it tower past the light pole until it disappeared into the dark summer sky, still ascending as it left our view. How cool! There were no outfield fences on most of the real fields we played on, and the ones that had them were typically placed too far away for any of us to knock one out of the park. So when we hit a homerun, it was usually because the ball kept rolling far beyond the outfielder and we were able to round the bases and stomp on home plate before the outfielder could fire the ball back in. This first tennis court homerun was a lot more fun to hit and watch, and it felt a lot more like the Cubs games we watched on WGN television from Wrigley Field in Chicago—another place known for easy homeruns when the wind was blowing out. We were intrigued with the possibilities that this new venue offered.

We finished the ride home on our bikes that night, thinking of how we might modify play a bit more to make the game more competitive, yet still be able to have a pretty good chance of knowing what it felt like to knock one out of the park and trot the bases slowly like Ernie Banks, Ron Santo, and Billy Williams did on TV. We all grabbed Popsicles out of the freezer at 116 when we got home and slurped them while sitting out in the yard on the limestone wall, calculating how the new game should be configured. We settled on the following: Rather than using a real baseball that could be hit too hard at someone in a small space and was too easy to hit a long distance, we adopted a kitty ball as the official game ball. A kitty ball was about five times bigger than a normal baseball and stuffed with something much softer than the core of a baseball. No gloves were needed to catch or field a kitty ball because it was more soft than hard. And finally, a kitty ball could only be hit about one third the distance a baseball would travel. We couldn't wait for the next day to go back to the tennis court and try out our new concept.

It felt peculiar the next morning, when we all gathered at 116 to go for our daily morning game of baseball without our gloves on the bike handlebars, which was a ritual. All we needed were a couple of bats and the kitty ball. We were downsizing before it was considered fashionable. When we arrived at the tennis court around nine a.m., we could not believe our eyes. A man and a woman had mustered the nerve to occupy our newfound baseball stadium with a couple of rackets and a small green and fuzzy ball that they were batting back and forth over the net. Obviously, they had missed out on Bakes' breathtaking, towering shot over the fence last night and had no concept of what this court's highest and most purposeful use was all about. We leaned our bikes against the fence and peered through its gaps, fingers wrapped around the metal weaving that constituted the enclosure. We thought by staring at the pair on the court and using our grip to rattle the fence once in a while, they might get the hint that we felt it was our turn to share the public area, but they did not catch on. After about ten minutes of hearing the tennis score called out first by her, then by him, Craig Demoss shouted out, "Hey! How long you guys plan on playing?" to which the woman replied, "I'm just about to finish him off. It's forty-love now." We knew how much forty was, but to our knowledge, 'love' was not a number. Regardless, we understood the gig was about up. Thank God.

When the tennis match was over, we could hardly contain ourselves as we huddled around the gray metal swinging gate that allowed access to the court. This couple, however, seemed to take forever putting the rackets away in their zippered covers, dropping the balls into the cylinder-shaped can, one at a time, and changing their shoes. The shoes were our limit. We swung open the gate and rushed the court, whisking by the preppy duo. It was time to play ball!

We had brought a piece of cardboard with us, which was placed at an angle in one corner of the court to represent home plate. We tore another piece off and placed it about fifteen paces away from the plate as first base. The two metal posts that served as bookends for the net became second and third. We agreed that runners didn't have to stand on them but did have to hold on to them with one hand; anyone who let go was considered off base and could therefore be tagged out. It wasn't long, however, before we began getting into verbal sparring sessions with tennis players over use of the court, and they tended to think what was off base was wanting to play baseball on a tennis court in the first place.

There were many such encounters. Some people were patient and allowed us the sixty-minute limit that was posted as the rule if other players were waiting to play. Others screamed at us, and we back at them. The most uncompromising of situations arose when a father and his son came to play tennis and tried interrupting our seven-inning game that was only in the top of the third. The dad was such a jerk that he told the son to take the court. He assumed his position on the other side of the net, and they commenced with a tennis game smack in the midst of our baseball game. It was a stubborn standoff, and no one would flinch. The tennis ball whizzed by the heads of our infielders, positioned by the net. Our base runners ran in what we considered the base path and barreled right into the path of the tennis players, shouting "Runner!" as they almost collided. This went on for an inning or two, until we finally decided it was no longer fun. We did leave our nemesis a parting gift though. When we departed, Dave Pierotti slipped the father's car keys that had been lying on the cement near his towel and racket cover, into his pocket. Dave tossed them into the open window of the guy's car. We're sure, however, the way things probably played out after our departure was that the tennis players thought they had lost the keys and looked around for a long while before finding them on the back seat of their Dodge Challenger. Serves ya right, tennis dad!

CHAPTER 18

Tree Heist

Just for the record, it should be noted that our neighborhood gang were not the only ones to misuse the Booth Street tennis court. In fact, the Young Men's Christian Association (YMCA) Volunteer Board was also guilty of this heinous crime—at least in November and December, when no one in Iowa plays tennis.

As part of their annual fundraising efforts, the Dubuque YMCA sold Christmas trees, starting the day after Thanksgiving and going through Christmas Eve. For that month-long period, the tennis court became a Christmas tree lot. Not even Charlie Brown would have thought of that one. The court was the perfect place for the trees. There was a fifteen-foot fence around it. A chain and padlock secured the gate at night, and the lights remained on for the viewing pleasure of potential purchasers of the seasonal green tannenbaums until eleven p.m. Perfect.

One season, on the Sunday evening of Thanksgiving weekend, a group of us were wandering around the tennis court turned Christmas tree farm, getting into the spirit of the season. It was around November 27 or 28, and our favorite time of year was fast approaching. As we wandered through the tree lot, Johnny Lyness suggested we should return that night, after eleven, when the lights went out, and steal a tree.

We answered almost in unison, "Duh, Johnny. They lock this place at night with a padlock and chain, Sherlock."

"Fine;" Johnny replied. "I'll bet you all five bucks I can climb the fence and throw a tree over the top and drag it home tonight."

Every one of us wanted a piece of this action until Steve, John's older brother, came to his defense and told him he was a fool and was about to lose all of his paper route money for the next two months.

At that, my brother Tom, who was known to have a competitive personality, rolled out an ingenious suggestion. "How about a team challenge?" he said. Within minutes, it was the Neuhaus and Schute brothers on one team; the three Pierotti brothers and Mark McLaughlin the second and the Lyness boys, Bakes and Craig DeMoss rounding out the third. The plan was for each of the three teams to meet at the tennis court at eleven thirty that night, with the objective of being the first team to get a tree out of the enclave. The bet was five bucks per team member, for a total of twenty big ones. Game on!

Bedtime for most of the gang was between nine and ten p.m. on school nights, so the first challenge was to figure how to slip out of our homes at the set time. Next came the problem of what tools might be required to assist in pulling off the caper and where we might access them. There was a lot to consider. We all went home to join in our family dinners, complete our homework, and then go to bed—except we had no intention of doing that.

After homework was completed at 116, Tom and I retreated to our bedroom as normal and bid our parents, "Sweet dreams." We figured Ken and Mary, old as they were, would be hitting the hay themselves after the ten-o'clock news, and there was a convenient ground-level window in our downstairs bedroom for easy access out and back in without anyone hearing doors open and close. We had rounded up some twine, scissors, and a pulley from Dad's tool area in the basement earlier that evening, so the materials were in order. Our primary challenge was staying awake until eleven fifteen, when we needed to slip out in order to be at the YMCA tree court by eleven thirty.

In our room, with the lights out, we listened to Top 40 songs on WDBQ radio for a while, until the old-time Sunday evening radio show, hosted by Bill Zwack, came on. We really liked listening to old-time radio programs that had been recorded in the days before television, and Zwack replayed them every Sunday night as a novelty for younger listeners and a nostalgia trip for the older ones. As we lay in our beds talking back and forth while listening to the *Fibber Magee and Molly* show, I noticed that Tom had gone somewhat quiet. I called his name, but there was no response. I listened closer, and a snore could be heard coming from his side of the room. Tom had crashed out on me! I gazed at the sweep hand on the 1970's version radio alarm clock (a staple in our small array of bedroom furnishings); it was approaching eleven. I got out of bed, crawled over to Tom's bed without turning on a light, and roused him from the haze that had fallen over him. Within minutes, we were both dressed in dark clothing, including dark stocking caps. We reached under my bed and pulled out our Christmas tree theft accessories, then, like some kind of reverse burglary attempt, climbed out our bedroom window.

Mark McLaughlin was already standing in the late November frosty and frozen grassy area between 116 and his house, waiting for Tom and me, when we completed the cautious and silent closing of our bedroom window. We were careful to leave it unlocked, as it would be necessary to make a hasty re-entry after we had won the Stolen Christmas Tree Competition of 1973. The three of us headed through several back yards en route to the tree court, careful to avoid being spotted in the glow of the occasional streetlight by any neighborhood adults that might still be awake. These were still the days when neighbors talked to one another regularly and felt a mutual responsibility to report any mischief by one another's kids to the appropriate other parent.

When we arrived at the tree court, only about two-thirds of the gang had actually showed up. Some likely fell asleep, while others' planned exits may have been foiled by insomniac parents who refused to turn in for the night. It was the Schute brothers, Tom,

Mark, and me. There were no Pierotti or Lyness brothers. Johnny, the founder of the idea, even stood us up, and as far as we were concerned, that was just wrong.

In short order, we concluded the competition should be called off, and we all agreed it would be best to fold the group into one cohesive unit focused on a shared objective: Pull an improbable Christmas tree heist from the Young Men's Christian Association stock, in a style that would put even the Grinch who stole Christmas to utter shame.

Being the most athletic and best climbers among the group we had, the Schute brothers were elected to scale the tall fence and serve as inside operators. Craig DeMoss and Bakes were husky, stronger types, so they were assigned the outside pulling duties. Mark, Tom, and I decided we would best serve the group by acting as lookouts, each in charge of keeping an eye out in different directions for any oncoming traffic, pedestrians, or—God forbid—cops. Operation Tree Heist went into motion, with the Schutes up and over the fence as though they' had done it a hundred times. The three lookouts were at our posts, and the brawn of the bunch ran twine through the pulley and then tossed the whole ball of burlap-smelling cord over the fence for the Schutes to utilize at their discretion. Tom and Mike were busy wrapping twine around the trunk of a tree and reinforcing it multiple times on a number of the evergreen limbs to ensure adequate strength, when a car suddenly turned the corner off of Dodge Street and onto Booth Street, right in front of the tree court.

As it completed its turn onto Booth, it slowed to barely an idle, and on came a spotlight that scanned the tree court. It was indeed a team of Dubuque's finest. Those of us on lookout dropped to the ground and froze. The Schutes both slipped into the little wooden warming shed that the volunteer workers used during regular hours to escape the chill of the season, where they kept the cash box. Craig and Bakes ran into the woods that bordered the court on the side where they were perched. A still silence prevailed in the cold air. I was shivering as I lay on the November earth, not sure if it was from fear or the temperature or perhaps a little of both. I noticed the twine that the brawny guys had let go of, still dangling over the outside of the fence near me. If the spotlight caught this, it was sure to bring the officers out of their car for a closer look. Much to our relief, within a minute that seemed like an hour, the blue police cruiser turned off the light and picked up speed as it moved on down the block to continue what appeared to have been their routine nightly rounds. We later concluded that all they probably looked at was the chain and padlock on the gate, and seeing it in place had satisfied their somewhat lazy, but dutiful, curiosity. We all stayed still a few more minutes and then mutually agreed via a quiet, blind shout out to each other that it was time to call off the operation. We all headed different directions home to avoid the appearance of a crowd or conspiracy of any type.

When Tom and I got to our bedroom window, and bid Mark Mac a goodnight, we were startled as we pulled upward on the bedroom window; it would not budge. It did not seem cold enough out that it could have frozen shut, so we pulled a bit harder. A harsh realization hit me: Someone had locked the window during the thirty or so minutes we had been gone.

We walked around to the front door of the house, where we could see that the kitchen light was on. There at the table, re-reading the Sunday newspaper as a way to pass time, was big Ken. We knew who had locked the window, and we knew we were busted. There was no alternative but to ring the doorbell and take our punishment. We brainstormed a bit, trying to come up with some plausible explanation as to what had prompted us to climb out the window, but we struggled to find anything that sounded the least bit reasonable. For a moment, we wondered if somehow Dad had caught wind of our tree adventure. I wondered, *Should I tell the truth or lie?* I opted for the latter. We could always go to confession and have it waived off our record.

Ding-dong went the bell, and up from his chair rose Big Ken. I don't even remember what we tried to pass off as our reason for slipping out the window, but it was an obvious lie, and the old man knew it. He was pissed that we held out on him and never told the truth, so he grounded both of us for a month. Even after all that went on that night, to think we didn't even snag a tree.

CHAPTER 19

Sherwood Forest

The tree-filled woods that bordered the Booth Street tennis court provided a rustic playground for what, at the time, appeared to us to be a wilderness area—the new frontier. It was the kind of place Daniel Boone or Huck Finn would have loved to explore and tame. We called the area Sherwood Forest, though as far as I can recall, it had no official name.

Our Sherwood Forest occupied about forty acres of space between Booth Street and Grandview Avenue going east and west and Dodge Street and Parkway to the south and north. Whenever we planned to spend a day in Sherwood, we knew it would be a full one. We headed out around nine a.m. and knew we wouldn't be home until six or seven p.m. The checklist, before setting off from 116, would include: BB guns; a yellow and black thin wax-coated cardboard carton that resembled a quart container of milk, filled with about 1,000 Daisy brand BBs; sack lunches; water-filled metal canteens wrapped in green canvas pouches that had been purchased at the Army surplus store; and an assortment of tools (a couple of handsaws, hammers, a good long strand of rope, a garden shovel, and plenty of nails).

When we arrived in the woods, the first order of business was usually to begin blazing a trail into a territory that had been relatively unexplored. There were about five main trails that received enough regular traffic to keep them cleared, but the rest of the woods were pretty dense with trees and foliage, and plant life grew so fast in there that even the main trails were quick to become overgrown with something green if not used over the course of a just few weeks.

We blazed new paths by swinging our saws and garden shovels in a pendulum-type motion, low to the ground. The five or six of us that were normally out together walked single file as we blazed so that whatever the first guy didn't clear, the second guy did, and what the second guy didn't, the third guy did, and so on. By the time the last guy completed his pass through an area, it was pretty well cleared.

After trailblazing lost its appeal, we would load our BB guns and take some target practice at tree branches, leaves, or perhaps a squirrel, rabbit, or bird that might come into view. It would also not be out of the ordinary to split up into two teams and shoot at each other. One team would close its eyes and count to 100, while the other team would wander off into the woods, set up in an ambush location and wait for the pursing team members to expose themselves to sniper fire. The pursing team would have to try and shoot all of the ambushers before the ambushers could shoot all of them. We saw way too many Vietnam War clips on the nightly news and way too may war movies in the theatres. We were fed the glorified and heroic aspects of war by the media, and we bought into it hook, line, and sinker. For us, war was a game . . . and it was a fun one.

After a few rounds of combat, more often than not, someone would get shot too close to an eye or in the face, and recognizing the potential fallout of the game, we would retreat to alternative forms of amusement. If we had had football helmets to wear, I'm sure our war games would have gone on safely all day. Ken can certainly attest if no one else.

Most trips to Sherwood were capped off with the building of a tree house or fort. There were lots of downed tree limbs strewn throughout the woods, and if we ventured close enough to the Grandview Avenue boundary of the refuge, we could usually scrounge up some pieces of wood or other excess construction material people had backed up in their trucks and dumped at the edge of the woods. Our hammers, saws, nails, and rope, in combination with a whole lot of sweat, could produce in the course of about two or three hours a functional tree house or a fort of some type, in which we would all hang out for the remainder of the day. More often than not, it was an unspoken rule that lunch could only be eaten in the clubhouse, after its completion. Most of the structures we built lasted for about a month or so before they fell victim to a severe thunderstorm or flashflood. The exception, of course, was when they became vandalism targets of the rival neighborhood gang from the nearby Parkway neighborhood, with whom we only interacted when we wanted to challenge them to a baseball game or go-kart race. Fort and tree house destruction sometimes seemed to outpace our ability to build them. Whenever we entered Sherwood and found one of our dwellings had been trashed, we wandered through the woods until we found one our foes had built, and retaliated by trashing theirs. These disputes escalated until the ultimate act of disrespect occurred.

Gene Ray, Jimmy Wagner, the Decker brothers, the Langas brothers and the Kieffer brothers pretty well constituted the core of the Parkway neighborhood gang. Over the course of several weeks, they had cleverly constructed a pretty elaborate tree house/deck platform, with a rope ladder that could be dropped down and pulled back up through a hinged trap door in the floor of the structure. Near the platform, tied to an extended tree limb, was a rope swing that the boys could run and grab onto, then swing back and forth high above the forest like Tarzan until it lost momentum and guided them back to the platform. Also, stashed in their elaborate king of all boy-built structures, was something few of us had seen but had heard gossip about plenty of times. It was the stuff of adolescent urban legends: a copy of *Playboy* magazine.

After entering the woods on three consecutive days, only to find our forts from each of the previous days completely trashed, we had tolerated all we could. Mad as we could be, we headed for the kingly estate, revenge on our minds. When we got to the enemy structure, the rope ladder had been foolishly left hanging by the last Parkway guy who had used it. Ken climbed the rope ladder faster than I had ever seen him move, grabbed the *Playboy*, and scurried back down the rope ladder. When his second foot stepped down onto the forest ground, he reached into his belt, next to his canteen, and pulled from its leather holster that slid on and off of his belt a six-inch, razor-sharp hunting knife. Fearing Ken was going to make some kind of sacrifice of the beautiful publication, Tom Schute began to plead with Ken to let him glimpse through the pages of hot and scantily clad young women. Ken said, "Hang on to this," and handed the nudie magazine into Tom's eager hands. At that, Ken scampered back up the rope ladder and proceeded to slash the rope where it connected to the platform, sending the heavy material into a free fall to the ground, where it landed with a *thud* in a coiled snake-like pile. We took the rope ladder and the *Playboy* with us as we headed to the other end of the woods, near the Booth Street tennis court. We stashed the rope and the magazine in a high pile of brush for future reference. Good luck getting back into your clubhouse, Parkway boys. Ya should have thought about that before you messed with the Nevada boys' forts!

CHAPTER 20

Urban Sprawl and the Mall

At some point around the time I was entering the fifth grade, while we were apparently not paying much attention, the YMCA/YWCA bought the wooded property we had always thought of as our personal playground. They were quick to bring in the bulldozers to eliminate our precious Sherwood. Within a matter of weeks, our beloved forest was about seventy percent leveled. We wondered if the people who operated the old Y had found out we were messing with their Christmas trees and this was their idea of getting even. It was a bit more drastic measure of revenge than cutting a rope ladder or stealing a nudie magazine, or so we thought anyway. The lyrics of a Joni Mitchell tune that was popular at the time seemed to characterize what we were feeling and seeing happen in our own back yard: "They paved paradise and put up a parking lot . . ." Joni hit the nail on the head.

By the start of sixth grade, Sherwood, as we knew it, was toast, and a beautiful modern brick and glass YMCA/YWCA covered the hallowed ground that had spawned some of the best adventures of our youth. When the Y built a fort, they <u>really</u> built a fort! The new Y had three basketball courts that could be separated by huge plastic/

vinyl sliding curtains. It had an oversized indoor pool, complete with a high dive, low dive, and starting platforms. It had brand new locker rooms and showers, complete with these really cool electric blow dryers on the wall that we could dry our hair under before going out into the winter cold. We had never seen anything like them. Completing the lower lever of the new playground for adults and youth alike were a weight room and four handball and racquetball courts. Upstairs was the arts and crafts room, a pre-school, as well as a game room with pool tables, bumper pool tables, game tables, foosball, and some other cool stuff. There was even a big pool observation room, with huge glass picture windows that allowed up to about fifty people to view the entire pool area one story below. Whatever loyalty we had to Sherwood and whatever nostalgia we clung to at first evaporated in record time when we feasted our eyes on the new Y. We all had our membership cards the first day they were available, and we used them . . . a lot!

While we were completely blindsided by the demolition of Sherwood Forest, perhaps we shouldn't have been. There were a number of indications that, as Bob Dylan observed, "The times, they are a changing." Bob was right.

The opening of the Y introduced a number of changes to life as we had known it. One aspect we found interesting was how the new facility became a social melting pot that crossed many neighborhood and school boundary lines. Prior to the new Y opening, about the only time we ever saw kids from outside our neighborhood or schools was during summer baseball challenges or when we competed against one another in sports during the school year in the Catholic school league. The Y became a magnet for kids from all areas of town, Catholic schools and public alike, drawn by all it had to offer. Some Friday nights, dances would be held in the gymnasium or teens had swim parties in the pool area. Occasionally, they had lock-ins, all-night sleepover parties when anyone in the building at ten p.m. one night would be locked in until eight a.m. the next morning. We wandered the building all night long, having a variety of fun with a whole new blend of people we otherwise would have had little reason to meet or get to know. It was an introduction to the expanded world of people we were ultimately destined to connect with when we reached high school, so it became a preview, of sorts, of things to come.

In the earliest years of our youth, most all of Dubuque's major retail commerce took place in the downtown area. The department stores—Stamphers, Sears, Montgomery Wards, JC Penney, and the daddy of them all, Roshek's, which was housed in its own ten-story full block building—were all within just blocks of one another in the downtown area. I recall getting in the elevator at Roshek's around Christmas time when I was a small boy. There was a lady who sat on a swivel stool inside the elevator and operated the control panel. She would swing an accordion-style gate open to let you on, ask what floor you wanted as she closed the gate, and then up you went. Imagine that was someone's job! We would go to the record department at JC Penney to make our purchases though. No kid ever bought entire vinyl albums containing all of a recording artist's music, but rather 'forty-fives', as they were called—the ancient version of what would be known as a 'single' on cassette, years later. We could buy our favorite songs on a piece of vinyl no bigger than a saucer or small kitchen plate, and it only cost ninety-nine cents at JC Penney. The flipside had another song by the same artist on it, but rarely did we ever want to listen to the other side. We knew which forty-fives to buy because we listened to Casey Kasem's *Top 40 Countdown* on WDBQ Radio for about four hours on Sundays and then rushed to Penney's later that week to buy the coolest new song for our collection at home. Downtown was where the stores were, just as plain as the church is where Mass was.

Around 1968 or 1969, that all began to change. A developer teamed with the City to clear a couple hundred acres of farmland on the west edge of town to build Kennedy Mall, the region's first indoor, multi-shopping conglomerate. Instead of taking the bus downtown to hang out or buy new clothing at the start of the school year, we would hop on the expanded Keyline bus route that now headed west to an area that not much earlier had only produced corn and soybeans. National chain stores we never heard of were all lined up indoors, next to one another—places like Spencer Gifts,

Things Remembered, and Trouser Works. And forget the old record department down at JC Penney. Musicland was at the mall and had eight-track tapes and vinyl LPs with five or six songs on each side, all by the same artist. Yeah, times, they were a changing. Even the days of going downtown to one of the old movie houses to see the latest release at the Grand, Orpheum, State, and the Strand were to be over soon. The cinema at the mall had about six theatres, with a different movie showing in each one. More appeared to be better, and Kennedy Mall definitely had more. If more did not appeal to someone, they shopped there anyway. After all, the place was named after the recently assassinated, greatest president of our time, John F. Kennedy . . . and out of respect of him, if nothing else, Kennedy Mall kept very, very busy.

CHAPTER 21

Pixie Shmixie!

My parents had four boys and four girls during their productive, Catholic-governed, sexually active years. I had three older sisters and one younger, two older brothers and one younger.

When my three older sisters, Mary Lynn, Patsy, and Cathy were young, they were Girl Scouts. My mother Mary was a troop leader. One summer when Tom was six or seven and I was four or five, Mom and my sisters had a whole week of Girl Scout day camp at Eagle Point Park on the far north end of the city. It had hundreds of treed acres that sat high above the Mississippi River on the bluffs overlooking Lock and Dam 11. The lock and dam system, designed and constructed in the 1930's, was a project of the Depression Era Great Society Program, which was intended to stimulate the economy by creating government-funded projects. The lock and dam system's purpose was to control the ebb and flow of the mighty Mississippi and aide in flood control efforts. The dam holds the water back, and flow is restricted and permitted by the opening and closing of the massive metal doors that comprise it from the north limits of Dubuque on the west side of the river, across to the southern Wisconsin state line, which borders the northern edge of the Illinois state line on the east side of the river. We often went to the park to watch from above as the barges navigated through the locks.

Since Mom needed to be at the camp from seven a.m. until five p.m., Monday through Sunday, with my sisters and their troop, Tom and I were required to go along each day and take part in what was called the Pixie Program. What a Pixie is exactly, Tom and I did not—and to this day still do not—know. All we knew is that we did not want to be one. In essence, the Pixie Program was a babysitting service provided by senior Girl Scouts for people like my mother who needed someone to watch their other kids while they mentored the young ladies on the merits of Girl Scouting. My mother was good that way. She was also a Den Leader for all four of her boys' Cub Scout packs.

It was only a few hours into the first day of being Pixies when Tom and I both observed that of the twenty or so kids in our group; there were about seventeen girls, Tom, me and just one other boy. That other boy seemed like Pixie material, as he liked to jump rope and wear the girls' barrettes in his hair. Even though we didn't know what it meant to be gay, we instinctively thought he fit the bill. I couldn't help but wonder what they were trying to do to my brother and me. We didn't want to catch gay or cooties or whatever else made a boy like jump rope and barrettes.

All week long, we were forced to do girly activities. Given the choice, we would have rather had hot pokers from a campfire stuck in our eyes, but it wasn't about choice. We were captives, prisoners of a benevolent dictatorship. "Hop scotch, anyone? Now sing 'Skip to my Lou' while you hold hands with your partner." The other boy wanted to be Tom's partner. For a moment, I was entertained and laughed at the thought, but I was abruptly brought back to the harsh reality of Pixie Camp when the next activity time arrived and we were instructed on the fine art of braiding hair. Yuck!

To make matters worse, we even had to go public in onstage performances. They made us do it again each day all week long. We did not know it at the time, but we were rehearsing a performance that would be presented to the Girl Scouts and troop leaders at the close of camp on Sunday afternoon.

To this day, some forty-five years later, I cannot get the words of one song they made us sing out of my mind . . .

"Oh Dubuque, Oh Dubuque how ya make me shiver, with yer tall green grass and yer Mississippi River, oh I love ya with my heart and I love ya with my liver, oh Dubuque, by the river!"

Throughout the week, I was partnered with the same girl, Salina. I was made to sing with her, hold hands with her, and dance with her in preparation for our impending performance. She loved every minute of it and developed a huge flirty crush on me. Trust me when I say the feelings were not mutual.

We had to do this act where we sang a little song, then turned rump to rump and gave each other a gentle bump, rump to rump, and then we proclaimed the ending phrase, "Ahkee ah!" with one final gentle rump bump. When Sunday came, and we were performing our show, pitiful moment by pitiful moment, I began to develop a plan for how I could pull off an open act of rebellion against all of this Pixie crap that had been shoved down our throats all week. When we got to the "Ahkee ah!" part and the final rump bump, instead of a gentle bump to Salina's rump, I laid a bump on her with such force she became airborne and flew headfirst into the lilac bushes about three feet off the edge of the stage. Next thing I remember, we were in the 1962 Buick wagon my father, Ken, drove to Torbert Drug most days, but not that Sunday afternoon. It was very quiet in the car, and after that day, we were never invited back to Pixie Camp again. Aw, shucks.

CHAPTER 22

The Family that Prays Together
Strays Together

Of my three older sisters, Cathy was the one closest in age and personality to me. She was three years my senior. Cathy was a lot of fun and was definitely the most tomboyish, rebellious girl in the house, as much as Patsy and Mary Lynn were conformists who did whatever Dad and Mom asked of them. Mary Lynn and Patsy sought recognition through adherence to standards and expectations. Cathy sought the same attention, but she usually accomplished it through defiance and misbehaving. Like I said, she was a lot more fun . . . and a lot more like me.

All of my parents' eight children attended Catholic grade school from grades one through eight. We also attended church together as a family up until about the time I entered the sixth grade. Around this time, the church introduced Saturday evening Mass, departing from the long-held tradition of Sunday-only services. I always assumed the new Saturday offering was instituted to allow the adults to get Mass out of the way before they hit the bars on Saturday night, thus preventing the need to get up with a hangover and attend—or worse yet, not attend at all. We were taught that missing church on Sunday was a super bad thing that would render your life empty and mark you as lower than low. The five-fifteen Saturday evening Mass became popular in record time. It was packed. As some of the older kids in the family took on part-time jobs, had more social engagements, family group attendance became a thing of the past. The new way of attending became an older sibling who could drive shepherding a few younger siblings to the service and back home. I preferred to attend with Cathy.

One Saturday evening, Cathy and I were the lone family members to head out of 116 bound for 5:15 Mass. We hopped in the sage green 1967 Buick Skylark two-door sedan and each took our places in our bucket seat. After life in a station wagon, we thought this car was totally cool and were thrilled my dad had picked it up to use as a second car for the growing family of drivers.

As we headed up Alpine Street, turning a quick right onto University Avenue, and then a quick left onto Alta Vista, we approached the Nativity School and Church parking lot. Rather than turning into the lot, Cathy drove right up to the front walk of the church and pulled the Skylark over. She put it in park and let it idle. I asked what she was doing, to which she replied, "Sit tight. I'll be right back."

I watched her walk up the sidewalk and in the door of the church, still confused as to what was up. Within seconds, Cathy was headed back down the walk toward the idling Buick, with a weekly church bulletin in her hand. The church bulletin was a simple sheet of white paper folded in half with the church logo printed on the front in black ink. It contained news blurbs and important dates for the week that involved the school and the parish. Typically, attendees grabbed a bulletin on their way out of Mass from the open wooden box that hung upright on the wall by the doors. It was unheard of to grab one prior to Mass.

Cathy opened the car door, moved the gearshift on the column to drive, and pulled away from the curb confidently, tossing the bulletin in the back seat.

"What are you doing?" I asked with some degree of anxiety and concern.

"We're skipping," she said, unfazed by my inquiry.

"You mean we're not going to Mass?" I questioned.

"That's right, bucko," she said. "We're outta here." And we were.

My emotions were mixed. I was thirteen years old and halfway through the seventh grade. I had not missed a Sunday Mass in my entire young life, except for a handful of times when I was exceptionally ill. We're talking a record of attendance that spanned something like eight years, since I was in kindergarten, over four hundred Sundays. And just like that, we were blowing it off. After getting past the initial reaction, which was incredible guilt (an emotion the Catholic Church prides itself upon) and fear of my parents or a nun at the school finding out, my mind opened to the thrill of the adventure. "So where we goin'?" I asked.

"Wherever you want," Cathy answered. "We gotta burn an hour and fifteen minutes."

I turned the radio in the Skylark up loud. Cathy and I headed down Loras Boulevard with the windows open, the fresh spring air blowing in our faces. We were singing, in unison, the Elton John hit, "Crocodile Rock" that was blasting from the car speakers. I was struck by a profound sense of freedom, of being a grownup. Life had changed forever. We had crossed over to the other side. We were coming of age in Iowa and were no longer going to be controlled by the Church or our parents. Game on!

When we observed that five-fifteen had turned to six-thirty, it was time to return to 116. We pulled up in front of the limestone rock wall on Solon Street, and Cathy turned the wheels on the Skylark in toward the curb and turned off the ignition. The joyride had temporarily taken away my initial sense of guilt, but I was getting nervous now about going in the house and facing my parents and lying to them about something so important to the value system they had instilled in us. Cathy appeared to have no problem at all, and from her nonchalance, I gathered this was not the first time she had skipped. As we opened our respective doors to exit the car, she instructed me to reach in the back seat, snatch up the church bulletin that had been tossed there at the outset of our charade, and place it prominently on the kitchen table where all family members passing by that high-traffic area of the house could see undeniably that we had, indeed, been to church. Cath, without a doubt, was not a rookie when it came to skipping . . . or deception, for that matter.

Needless to say, my sister Cathy and I became regular church mates. When I shared our little secret with Mark McLaughlin and the Schute boys, they persuaded their folks to let them attend church with Cathy and me. They, too, returned home each time with a church bulletin, having been taught well by one of the best in the Mass-skipping business.

Cathy also had an interesting approach to penance, or confession, as we more commonly referred to it. Penance is one of the Seven Sacraments utilized to indoctrinate young people into the Catholic faith. When a child reaches the age of ten or eleven, they are welcomed to a new level of membership in the Church that provides for them the opportunity to practice the ritual of penance that is intended to cleanse their sinning soul and relieve their guilt-ridden conscience. Inside all Catholic churches is an area or several areas known as confessionals. The confessional at Nativity consisted of two telephone booth-sized private, enclosed areas. There was a solid wooden door on each booth. One booth was for the priest, and the other was for the confessor. The priest entered his booth before the confessors appeared in line at the confessor's booth, so the priest never saw who was lining up to confess. When the confessor entered his or her booth and closed the door behind them, they would find themselves in a confined and dark area with no windows or light. There was a cushioned vinyl kneeler about two feet long and eight inches wide pressed up against the base of the solid wall that separated the priest from the church member. After the priest could sense that someone had entered the confessor side of the booth, he would slide open a small opaque screen in the center of the common wall. While not allowing any visual contact, the opaque screen did allow for audio transmittal between the priest and his subject. The scripted routine went like this: Upon the sliding open of the screen, the confessor would state, "Bless me, Father, for I have sinned. My last confession was . . ." And then you would state how long it had been since your last confession. After establishing the timeframe, the confessor was then expected to itemize all the sins they had committed since the last time they had been to confession and verbalize them anonymously to the priest.

When the confessor had finished, the priest would reply with a tightly scripted response ending with an assigned battery of prayers the confessor was to recite in solitude out in the church after leaving the booth. The last thing the priest would say was something akin to, "With the power vested in me by the Catholic Church, I hereby absolve you of these and all of your sins. Now go forth to love and serve the Lord."

When penance is completed, confession forgives, or absolves you of your sins granting a clean slate. Generally, one was expected to attend confession at least once per month to stay cleansed.

As confession was a rather awkward and difficult exercise, it was often something we avoided for months on end, until the overriding guilt of something we had done compelled us to visit the dark, private booth to free our mind and spirit.

One day when I was talking with Cathy about how long it had been since I had gone to confession and the mounting anxiety I was having about revealing, even in secrecy to the priest, how long it had been between sessions, she offered an unthinkable, yet practical solution that she told me she used regularly. She stated, rather casually, "When you get to the part when you're supposed to say how long it has been, just lie."

"What?" I said with disbelief. "You can't lie to the priest when you're supposed to be confessing your sins! Lying is a sin, and that would be contrary to the purpose of confession."

"Although it's true, you are sinning when you lie to the priest," she said, "it's no problem because at the end, he says you are absolved of those and all your sins. The 'all your sins part' covers the lie, and you're good to go."

As irreverent as this sounded, I concluded my sister had found a handy technicality, a loophole nearly impossible to refute. I couldn't help wondering if anyone else used it.

CHAPTER 23

Driving Lessons

Another thing I enjoyed about my relationship with my third oldest sister was that she let me drive the car before I had a license. Sometimes I got to pilot the Skylark during our church outings, and other times, she let me drive her and her best friend Julie Spahn around town to various places on a Friday or Saturday night. It was so cool! Surely there was no better sister in the City of Dubuque—or probably the whole world for that matter.

While Cathy and I pulled a lot over Ken and Mary's eyes, they were not quite as naïve as I had begun to believe. I recall the first time I drove with my dad after I had received my learner's permit, midway through my freshmen year of high school. We were in the Skylark, and I had taken my position in the driver's seat for what he presumed to be was the first time ever. He insisted on instructing me on protocol. "Fasten your seatbelt. Adjust your seat. Manipulate the rearview mirrors until the view is customized to your needs. Place your foot on the brake prior to shifting the car into drive," and so on.

As we pulled from the curb and headed down Solon Street to the stop sign, I applied the touchy power brakes smoothly and evenly, bringing the car to a gradual stop just at the right location of the intersection. Back then, power brakes were hypersensitive, and it was not unusual for them to cause the car to jerk or stop abruptly if they were not applied properly. I dutifully executed my left turn signal and proceeded down Nevada Street to the next stop sign at Dodge Street, right in front of Frank and John's Gulf Station. Again, I performed the footwork on the sensitive power brakes to perfection. As we sat at the busy intersection of Dodge and Nevada and I flipped my left turn signal on, waiting for a break in traffic that would allow us access to the next desired direction, Dad ordered me to place the car in park. I thought this was odd, because I was certain that I had done everything perfectly and did not understand why he felt compelled to give me some type of criticism or pointer. As it turned out, that's not why he made me stop the car.

When I turned my head to the right to face Dad eye to eye, as he looked at me with a suspecting glare from his place in the instructor's seat, he blurted out, "This isn't the first time you've driven a car." He did not ask this as a question or with the slightest degree of inquiry. It was a brief, clear, and bold, all-knowing statement.

"Yes it is!" I lied, trying to convince him and myself of this untruth.

He shook his head and told me to proceed.

Great, I thought. I skip church regularly; drive without a license, and now I lie boldly to my father. I gazed past his face and noticed the Gulf Station logo to our right. One thought came to mind: Looks like Polka Dots is going to have some company in Hell.

Let the record be clear that I was not the only one of the Neuhaus boys to drive prematurely. In fact, compared to my oldest brother's early driving escapades, mine were quite benign. Although I was not old enough to remember the actual day of the forthcoming tale, I heard this told numerous times by various family members who were.

Being the bossy and in-charge kind of guy my brother Ken was, it was not surprising that if he were going to get into a car as a young boy, the only place for him would be the driver's seat. Such was the case one spring day back in 1961, when at the age of seven, he appointed himself to give Cathy and Tom (then ages six and four) a ride to school. Apparently, the three were outside playing, and Ken told Cathy and Tom to get in the 1957 Ford Fairlane that was then the family car. Keep in mind, my parents had told all of the kids never to play in the car and never to get in it without permission, but this was Ken, who was convinced that the rules about the car—like all rules—were for everyone but him.

Ken ushered Cathy and Tom into the back seat of the standard transmission sedan. He slammed the door and climbed into the driver's seat. Turning the steering wheel back and forth must have become uneventful for Ken, because after a few minutes of this underwhelming exercise, he opted to up the ante by pulling on the parking brake until it released. That was good for a while, but the ultimate excitement, Ken was convinced, had to be pulling on the stick shift. And let the excitement begin!

With Ken at the wheel and Cath and Tom ready for a big day of studying, the Ford began to roll slowly forward. Solon Street has a gradual grade in front of 116, and the car was going in the direction of the grade. When Solon crosses Nevada Street, however, it slopes quickly and dramatically down a steep hill. As the vessel proceeded across the intersection and began to pick up speed, its young captain, sensing danger, did what all good captains are trained to do: jump ship! Out bailed Ken, followed by Cathy. Tom, however, struggled to open his door as the car was now moving at a pretty good clip. A neighbor lady ran toward the runaway car and was able to pull Tom out, but he fell to the street and under the car, which proceeded to run over his legs and back. The Ford jumped a curb and was stopped when it plunged into the yard of our neighbor and Dubuque School Superintendant Joe Flynn. While Ken's intention was to get the kids to school, he really outdid himself by literally delivering them to the doorstep of the Headmaster himself! Tom was rushed to Mercy Hospital, but released the next day. It was a few days before he was able to walk again, but Tom quickly recovered. Ken's first time driving was frightening, but nonetheless, a predictor of things to come.

Ken's driving record did not improve much over the years. He owned exactly three cars between the ages of sixteen and twenty-one, and ended up wrecking exactly three cars during that same five-year period. I guess driving is just one of those things that comes with a lot of rules, and rules were never Ken's forte.

CHAPTER 24

My Sister, the Mayor

My oldest sister and first of Ken and Mary Neuhaus's children, Mary Lynn, suffered from an incurable case of oldest child syndrome. The symptoms of the disease, which in large part boils down to high expectations, include: too much reading, straight A's, little recreation, a requirement to become proficient at performing with a musical instrument, leadership roles in all extracurricular organizations and clubs that are not sports related, a career in law or medicine, and the ability to lie through your teeth in order to defend any perceived flaws that could otherwise damage the image of the perfect child. M.L., as we called her, covered all these bases with ease—particularly the last one, which may explain why she later became an accomplished lawyer.

M.L. was a gifted public speaker. She won many speech contests sponsored by local civic groups and participated as a key member of her high school and college debate teams. She also had a knack for politics and deal cutting. During the summer between her sophomore and junior years of college, much as a result of her networking abilities, she landed a great temporary job as the Director of the Dubuque Mayor's Summer Youth Employment Program.

The program was essentially a matchmaking clearinghouse where individuals and businesses that had low-level temporary work needs that could be performed by kids between the ages of sixteen and eighteen, could access a list of such candidates who had registered with the program, seeking summer employment.

Being the public servant and woman of the people that she was, and having studied and admired the political machine run by Chicago's famed, but corrupt Mayor Richard M. Daley, M.L. knew her first responsibility was to cherry pick the best jobs in town for her brothers. That's what Daley would have done, right?

It was the first week of June, and I had just finished the seventh grade, still thirteen years old. My brother Tom was fifteen and had completed his freshman year of high school. Neither of us were the required minimum age of sixteen, which was among the clearly stated rules for participation in the Mayor's Summer Youth Employment Program, the rules my sister was sworn to uphold. Perhaps it's worth noting here the irony of Ken, the oldest son, was named after my father, and Mary, the oldest daughter, named after my mother, insisted on breaking the rules. Or perhaps it's more of a pattern than irony.

One morning, as we sat in front of the TV at 116, watching Bob Barker on *The Price is Right*, the phone rang. It was M.L. She had found a job Tom and I could work on together. Minimum wage at the time was $1.10 per hour, but this job paid $2.00 per hour—big money, as far as we were concerned. She instructed us to get on our bikes and head downtown to the Mayor's Office right away so we could fill out some application paperwork before the job was posted for others to see. We were there in less than fifteen minutes. After a brief job interview with M.L.'s assistant (because M.L. did not want to appear to be acting with a conflict of interest in hiring her brothers), the assistant said we were right for the job. That assistant had quite an eye for talent, if I don't say so myself. She had just given the best jobs available to two guys who did not meet the minimum age requirement and who had not one ounce of experience in the line of work we would start later that day: painting the exterior of a three-story apartment building.

When we arrived at the big white apartment building near the top of West Third Street later that morning, Tom and I knocked on the door of the apartment occupied by the building manager, our boss in waiting. He answered the door and looked at us with a questioning look on his face. "Can I help you, boys?"

"Yes, sir. We have been sent here by the Mayor's Office to paint this building," Tom exclaimed.

"You boys done a job like this before, have ya?" the manager asked, looking at us a bit skeptically.

"Oh yes, sir," I replied without hesitation. "This is what we've done every summer since we started taking summer jobs." It wasn't exactly a lie; since it was the first time either of us had ever taken a real summer job.

"Okay. Follow me, and I'll show you where to start," said the manager.

And thus began what would become an ill-fated stab at the working world for Tom and me and a less-than-satisfying experience with the Mayor's Summer Youth Employment Program for the building manager.

About as close as Tom and I had ever gotten to painting a house was watching Dad do it at 116. The only thing we were experienced at was scraping and prepping the surface. Dad would give us these wood-handled scrapers with metal ends that curved under with a knob on the topside designed to allow you to grasp firmly and apply pressure to the scraping action. We pulled out our tools and began to scrape on the shaded side of the house, realizing this was going to be job security for the whole summer. As we scraped and toiled, we gazed up at the three-level apartment, wondering how we were ever going to reach the upper two levels. But there was plenty to be done on the main level, so we figured we would just cross that bridge when we got to it. We decided we would ask the manager to let us borrow some ladders or rent some for us. Of course, being the seasoned professionals we were, he assumed we would have brought those along ourselves.

After the end of the first week, we had pretty well scraped and used an eight-inch burner tool to peel and melt the old paint off the surface of the lower level of the house. At the rate we were going, we knew it was going take about a month just to prep the place for painting. At the start of the second week on the job, the manager came out to inspect our progress. He looked around and asked what progress we had made. When we pointed out that the lower third of the house was prepped and we needed him to go rent some ladders so we could start working in the second level, he informed us of two things. First, we did not need to be so thorough in our prep work, and second, the ladders were our responsibility.

Since neither one of us drove or had any money to rent ladders, we suggested to the manager that he pay us for the first week and give us a ride to a place we could rent ladders. He said he was only authorized by the owner to pay us once every two weeks and that it was not his problem that we did not have a way to get to the hardware store that rented ladders. Maybe it wasn't his problem at that moment, but it would be soon enough.

We knew there was a stepladder in the garage over at 116, so we walked home and together carried the ladder back to the job site. Tom and I discussed whether we should be paid for the time it took to get the ladder. We decided we should and made a note on our time card to that effect. When we got the ladder set against the side of the house, we could see it would not get us past the second level, but it was good enough for now. The manager came out and asked us how we were going to reach the third level with an eight-foot stepladder. We really had not the slightest idea, but we told him we had a bigger ladder at home and would bring that one when we were done with the second level. He informed us he was leaving to go on vacation for a week, and when he got back, he expected to see visible progress. We assured him he would.

Over the course of the second week, the prep work, which we continued to do the only way we knew how, got slower because of the fact we only had one ladder, and only one of us could get up on it at a time. It also had to be moved regularly, so there was a lot of time lost climbing up and down to move it. One afternoon, in order to make better use of our time, rather than one scraping from up on the ladder and one watching, I ventured up to the second floor apartment, for which we had a key, and entered it to gain access to a porch that extended out from the house. The plan was to climb out the window of the porch and walk along a rail that would allow me to access the lower part of the third level. As I wandered through the apartment toward the porch, I noticed a bag of Doritos (taco flavored, my favorite) on top of the refrigerator. Mark Jackson and Bill Lehman, two players for the Dubuque Packers Minor League Baseball team, occupied the apartment. Being one who followed the team, I knew they were on a four-day road trip and would not be home the rest of the week. I had missed lunch and was starving, so I didn't think they would miss a few of their Doritos. I unraveled the two-thirds full bag and scarfed a few down. About that time, Tom wandered into the apartment from outside to see how my efforts upstairs were coming. I pointed out the Doritos, and he helped himself to a handful of the crunchy delicacies. He passed the bag back to me, and I had some more. This went on until there were about six or eight chips left in the bag, along with some crumbs. We decided the bag needed to go back to its resting place, so we blew a little air into it, fluffed it up a bit, and put it back. The chips were salty, and we wondered if the absent Packers had anything in the pad to drink. We opened the fridge and found five cans of a six-pack of Pepsi. Tom and I decided we would split one. It was starting to resemble our assaults on the Schutes' place, but no one had even muttered the Search for Tomorrow code words before we started crunching and guzzling the stolen goods.

On the Monday of the third week, Tom and I showed up at the job site. The second level of the house had been about sixty percent prepped, and that was the extent of the progress since the manager had gone on vacation. He greeted us gruffly as we submitted to him our hours for the first two weeks of work, which tallied about ninety hours each, for a total of about $360. The manager was beside himself. He cursed us using every name in the book (and some I'm sure he invented) and told us our meager progress was completely inadequate. He fired us on the spot and ranted about how he would find someone else to do the job right.

We were fine with that, but we made sure to remind him of the timesheets for which we were already owed. As Tom pointed out the itemized hours in great detail, the manager looked at him like he was from another planet. The manager said, in essence, that what we did warranted no pay and we should beat it and forget about receiving any compensation. A little freaked out by this irate adult, Tom and I agreed it was time to retreat back to 116 with our stepladder and our ignored timesheets and lick our collective wounds.

Ten years of working on the loading dock at Torbert Drug had taken a toll on our Dad's back. Our neighbor a few doors down was Dubuque County Sheriff Johnny Murphy. As Tom and I had learned that summer, jobs often go to people based on whom they know, rather than what they know. We were more certain than ever after our painting episode that this was an absolute. The same was true for our dad, who was out cutting the grass one day when Sheriff Murphy stopped by in his squad car. He told Dad he was in need of a deputy and wondered if Ken knew anyone who would be interested. My dad said he did, and the next week, he came home from work in a squad car. Just like that, at age forty, our dad was a cop.

The first year Ken Neuhaus wore Badge 3109 for the Dubuque County Sherriff's Department, he was assigned the least desirable shift: midnight until eight a.m. He was low man on the totem pole, so to speak, but riding in a squad car was a lot easier on his back than lifting boxes of pharmaceuticals.

The day after Tom and I were fired, Dad came home from work around eight thirty a.m. and noticed we were still in bed. He stirred us awake, thinking we had overslept for our painting job. When we told him we had been fired and denied our pay, he was furious. "We'll see about that!" he said. He ordered Tom and me into the squad car to pay a visit to our former employer.

We pulled into the driveway at the big white apartment building in the white car with the red light bar on top, complete with a shotgun in the front windshield and big gold sheriff star decals on the driver and passenger doors. We all got out of the car and walked toward the door of the manager's apartment.

The manager must have noticed us out the window, because he stepped out before we could knock. Appearing rather nervous, he asked the officer what the problem seemed to be.

Ken Neuhaus, in his early middle years, was an imposing figure, particularly in full uniform. Without ever telling the man he was our father, the deputy proceeded to say, "These boys have reported to me that you owe them $360 for 180 hours of hard work, but you have refused to pay them. Is that true?"

"Well . . . not entirely," lied the manager. "I . . . I just have not had the opportunity to write the check yet. I can go in the house and get that taken care of right away, sir."

Two minutes later, the man handed Tom our check. We thanked him and returned to the authoritative car we arrived in, and before you could say "I want to paint your house," we had departed victoriously. This was the first of what would end up being a good number of times that Deputy Ken Neuhaus' occupation gave fringe benefits to his sons, and the trend continued, as we grew older.

CHAPTER 25

Uncle Donnie Takes a Dive

Dad was a child of the Great Depression. He had thirteen brothers and sisters, and as result, he found himself working to help support the family early on in his life. He dropped out of high school after the tenth grade and took a job on the hog kill line at the Dubuque Packing Company, where real money could be made. There was a small bar across from 'The Pack', as it was called by Dubuquers, that was run by Charlie Dugan. His daughter, Mary Julia Dugan, took work there as a young woman at the age of nineteen, keeping the books and serving shots and beers to The Pack's workers during their breaks and lunch hours. A few years later, when Ken was working as a Pepsi deliveryman, it was at Dugan's Tap that she met the man who would become her life partner. They married on Valentine's Day 1953.

Mary grew up under difficult circumstances. Her mother died of cancer when Mary was just a toddler of two or three years. My Grandpa Charlie enlisted the aid of his unmarried sister, Agnes Dugan, to help raise his only child at 116, a home that he and his sister originally owned together. Agnes was a schoolteacher and kept house for a Catholic priest. She and Mary bonded much the way a mother and daughter would for the rest of their lives. When Grandpa Charlie's health failed, Mary was called upon to take care of her father by moving back into 116 with Agnes, Charlie, Ken, and baby Mary Lynn. Charlie passed away in 1956, but the Neuhaus family was at 116 to stay, and Agnes welcomed her extended family with open arms. Agnes was an extreme Irish Catholic woman, proud of her religion and her ethnic heritage. Aunt Agnes was an omnipresent person in the lives of the Neuhaus kids as we grew up. She cooked, cleaned, ironed, read to us, and above all, made sure we prayed regularly before meals and on our knees before bedtime, looking at the crucifixes she hung in each bedroom in the house.

Whenever there was a threat or crises, Agnes would summon all of us together to pray. We would hear of a member of our school parish taking ill or having an accident, and she would gather us to pray for them. The tornado-warning siren would go off, and we would all end up huddled in the corner of the basement around Agnes, praying. There would be news of a young man from Dubuque who we did not even know being killed in the war in Vietnam, and we would pray for his family and the happy repose of his soul. We prayed about virtually anything and everything. Agnes made sure that when each of the four Neuhaus boys turned ten years old, we were enlisted as altar boys, to assist the priests in the serving of Catholic Mass at Nativity Church. Some weeks, we would be at six a.m. Mass each morning all during the school week, twice on Sunday.

One Agnes-directed praying marathon that will never leave my mind took place on a mid-spring evening when I was about four or five years old. I recall it was a school night, a Tuesday or Wednesday evening, and it involved one of Dad's brothers, Uncle Donnie. He was more a part of our lives growing up than most of Dad's other twelve siblings. Donnie was a plumber by trade, but his real passion was fishing the Mississippi River every minute he could, and he loved to hold fish fries for family and friends with his catches. Donnie drank a lot of Drewery's, Star, and Old Milwaukee beer, but truth be known, Uncle Donnie really only had two criteria when it came to choosing a beverage: cold and cheap.

On this spring evening around 1966, most of our family was gathered around the television or at the kitchen table completing our homework assignments when the phone rang. Mom answered it, and we all knew shortly by the grave look on her face and the tone of her trembling voice that whatever was being said to her by the person on the other end was not good news.

As my mother hung up the phone, a frantic look came over her face, and water glistened around both her eyes. She turned to my dad, and in a rushed and urgent manner blurted out, "That was Eunice [Uncle Donnie's wife]. You've got to get down to the Hawthorne Street boat dock immediately. The Coast Guard is dragging the river for Donald!"

Dragging the river was a fatalistic term heard regularly by anyone who grew up on the Mississippi. There were typically three or four drownings each summer season. The current of the river and the whirlpool-like movement in some areas of the mighty Big Muddy had a tendency to pull victims underwater. When conducting recovery operations, the Coast Guard would drop a big mesh net in the water and drag it around behind the recovery boat in the area where the victim was last seen, hoping to catch the dead body in the net. Just hearing about them dragging the river sent a chill through our veins . . . and this time, it was for one of our own.

As pandemonium ensued, Dad searched frantically for his car keys, with my mom walking hurriedly by his side like a shadow, everywhere he moved on his quest for the keys.

Taking command of the kids, as she so often did, Agnes directed all of us to circle around her swivel white vinyl rocking chair that was known by all of us as a place of comfort and stability. She began, "Children, we must pray to the Lord with all of our strength for Uncle Donald and ask that he be protected at this time." The pray-a-thon was on. Hail Mary's and Our Fathers, two standards in the Catholic prayer arsenal, were chanted continuously, in-group harmony, with the only interruption being an occasional breath. After about half an hour, the phone rang again, and Mom answered. A deafening silence fell over the entire house. We were all certain the news we were about to hear was that our much beloved Uncle

Donnie's body had been found. It was like a nightmare, and we all just wanted to wake up so it would be over, but that was not to be.

The call was an update from another of Dad's siblings telling us more about activities down at the Hawthorne Street boat dock, where Donnie kept his fishing boat. Aunt Nelda shared with Mom, that Donnie had been busy earlier that evening rebuilding the motor on the boat. Several people nearby had observed him there over the course of an hour or so. Eyewitnesses could place him at the scene up until about six thirty p.m., at which point he suddenly seemed to disappear with the boat motor, which he had successfully repaired, still running, the propeller treading water. It appeared likely he had somehow gotten caught in the propeller, cut up, and spit into the river. It was a gruesome, haunting visual, definitely far from good news. Our prayer session with Aunt Agnes fell utterly silent as Mom tearfully relayed the details to us about Uncle Donnie's likely fate. We felt as though there was not much point in continuing. Hope had turned to sorrow and grief.

Meanwhile, at the boat dock, the scene was that of an emergency. Red lights flashed from the fire trucks, Coast Guard vehicle, and police cars that had carried the rescue and recovery workers to the location of the incident. A reporter and photographer from the local newspaper were there, on task to record the tragedy for the next day's edition.

As the reporter wandered the area, seeking witnesses who could provide firsthand accounts of the events of the evening, a forty-something man with slicked back dark black hair and a Camel cigarette hanging from his mouth approached him. The man had come from the parking lot of a neighboring bowling alley and bar near the dock. Observing the commotion and dragging efforts and the grim looks on everyone's faces, the man asked the reporter, "Oh no! Did someone drown out here tonight?"

"Yes," replied the reporter, pointing to my Uncle Donnie's still idling boat. "The guy who owns that boat fell in and drowned about two hours ago. They're still trying to locate the body."

Just then, reports have it that my Aunt Eunice came running at the man who was engaged with the reporter, screaming obscenities.

When she reached him, she began to swing her fists at him wildly with every ounce of energy remaining in her grief-drained, small body, pounding at his chest. My Uncle Donnie then retreated from his wife, covering his face with both arms as his wife continued to chase him across the parking lot, back toward the bar. Our prayers had worked! God protected Donnie by guiding him into the bar for a few cold ones while his boat motor had time to get broken in. He had been saved from his believed ill fate. Hold the presses at *The Telegraph-Herald*! The only thing dead was this story.

As the story unfolded and Aunt Eunice's initial anger at her husband turned to relief and joy, Donnie explained that around the time he had finished with the motor rebuild, his buddy and fellow plumber, Lenny Backus, wandered by on his way to Riverside Bowl for a few beers. Since the last step in the process was to prime the engine by letting it run for a while, Donnie saw no harm in joining Lenny at the bar for a few, and that's where he had been the entire time the rest of Dubuque was writing his obituary. Much like Mark Twain, another river man, reports of my Uncle Donnie's death had been greatly exaggerated.

CHAPTER 26

Paula and Pat

I can remember the day my parents brought their newborn eighth child, my only younger sister, Paula, home from the hospital. It was September of 1967. I was six years old, sitting at the kitchen table eating a bowl of cereal, looking for some hokey prize that was advertised on the outside of the box, completely unaware that one of my older siblings had already nabbed it. Dad walked into 116 carrying a pink wicker-style bassinet, which he placed on the kitchen table. Thinking there might be something to eat in the basket because it resembled a picnic basket, I stood up on my chair, stretched my torso out over the table, and leaned my head over the basket with a probing eye. *Holy crap!* I thought. Somebody must have left a baby in a basket on our doorstep and my dad found it when he was coming up the walk. When I asked where the baby came from, he told me to ask my mom. When I asked Mom, she said it came from the hospital. When I asked if we were taking it back, they both said "No. It's ours . . . your new little sister Paula."

I wanted to say, "Okay, so what do we do with it . . . I mean her," but I thought better of it. I still wished there would have been something to eat in that big pink picnic basket instead.

As a few years passed and Paula got to be two or three years old, I played with her a lot, gave her quite a few horsey rides and that kind of stuff, pretended to be a dog for her, and played records she would dance and bounce around to until she would get dizzy and wipe out on the living room floor. Whenever she fell down, we both laughed hysterically. I don't know why, but it just seemed funny to both of us. A few years later, we were on a family outing to Chicago to visit some relatives and attend a Chicago Cubs baseball game at Wrigley Field, but for Paula, this experience became less than funny.

We were backed up in traffic on Addison Street, not moving at all in our quest to reach the stadium. After a four-hour drive, the van full of family members was getting a bit claustrophobic, and everyone was getting a little edgy. The van was at a standstill near the corner of Addison and Cornelia Streets. Paula, being a bit of a whiner and the somewhat spoiled youngest child who got what she wanted by throwing temper tantrums, was going on and on about something, and none of us were in the mood to be tolerant. Instead of succumbing to her demands, several of us concocted a crazy story to tell her, the premise being that she was not really a member of our family, that we had found her as a baby in a trashcan on Cornelia Street in Chicago, and that if she didn't shut up, we would stuff her back in the can she came from, just outside the van at the intersection we were at. We said she was adopted and we really didn't want her anymore, and I think one of us actually opened the van door in a veiled threat to make her believe we were really going to do it. Well, rather than shutting her up, the cruel story and threat of abandonment served to make matters even worse not only for the day, but in terms of her ability to trust some of her siblings for the next few years. We really should have gone to confession on that one.

The second oldest Neuhaus child was my sister Pat, or Patsy or Patti, depending on the year—always Patricia Ann when she was in trouble with the parents. By whatever name, she was the same steady, dependable, trustworthy, and overall stabilizing sibling influence that helped to offset a few that were not so much that way for a good number of years.

Pat spent a lot of her youth trying to keep up with the oldest brainiac and high-achieving daughter, Mary Lynn. For a number of years, Pat followed in a lot of Mary Lynn's footsteps: marching band, Junior Achievement, Student Council, early high school at the Catholic all-girls Visitation Academy, and more. Eventually, after I suspect she realized she could not or no longer cared to keep up with the oldest child, Pat took on her own identity, group of friends, social activities, and the like. Her transformation seemed to coincide with a boyfriend she brought home by the name of Rob Jones. They were in the theatre group and choir together at the public high school she transferred to when The Viz closed. Little did we know at its outset that this was a relationship that would set off a firestorm of controversy in our house. The absence of Catholic education, as we would soon overhear at 116, could be the only explanation at the epicenter of this girl gone wild. The grown-ups in our lives were certain that if Pat had gone to the Catholic high school, Wahlert, she would have met a nice Catholic boy, something Rob Jones definitely was not.

Not long after they started dating, Rob and Pat became famous for lying on the living room couch at 116 and making out blatantly without regard for how many of the younger kids might be in the same room watching television. Their raging hormones kept them oblivious to anyone or anything else going on around them when they went into smooch mode. My Great Aunt Agnes, the die-hard Catholic was on Rob's case from day one because not only did Rob attend a Methodist church in town (I think there may have been two at the time), but also his mother was even the organist there. Aunt Agnes considered this high treason, and she wanted the smooching 'dirty Methodist' out of the house. I often overheard the spirited debate between her, Pat, and my parents even hours after Rob had left to go home. Despite the protests, and with some recognition of and adaption to the sensitivities that existed, all parties eventually forged a compromise, and about six years later, Pat and Rob were married.

CHAPTER 27

Say It Ain't So, Joe

When our dad began his career in law enforcement in the summer of 1969, he was the ninth deputy hired into the department. His badge number, 3109, referred to two things. First, the state of Iowa has ninety-nine counties. Each is assigned a numerical identifier, and Dubuque's was 31. Being the ninth deputy in the department, 09 represented his tenure with the force. The Chief Deputy, Badge 3102, was held by a kind, aging gentleman by the name of Walter Hoerner, whom my dad reported directly to in his early years with the department.

Walter Hoerner had three sons. The middle one, Joe, was one of the few people—if not the only person from Dubuque—to be able to claim status as a more heralded baseball player than Kevin Rhomberg. Although Joe was a journeyman left-handed relief pitcher in the big leagues, playing a combined fourteen seasons for the parent clubs of the St. Louis Cardinals, Atlanta Braves, Philadelphia Phillies, and the then-expansion Kansas City Royals, he was Dubuque's claim to fame for a number of years. Walter could not have been more proud of his son, particularly when he made several appearances for the Cardinals in the 1967 and 1968 World

Series' against the Boston Red Sox and Detroit Tigers, and when he was selected for the National League All-Star team as a member of the Philadelphia Phillies in 1970.

In the summer of 1975, just before I entered high school, part of our family went on a summer vacation together. Much like what happened to family churchgoing around that time, some of the family had commitments to sports, summer school, jobs, and so on and could no longer take part in the family getaways. On this particular summer trip, it was only my parents, Mary Lynn, my brother Greg, my younger sister Paula, and me. We set out in the 1970 Ford Club Chateau van (which turned out to be the last family car we all rode in together), pulling the Nomad traveler trailer that would become our home for a two-week tour of Missouri, to include a lot of time around the Lake of the Ozarks and stops in St. Louis and Kansas City.

Joe Hoerner was playing that summer, albeit in the second to last year of his career with the Kansas City Royals. His career was winding down, and he had been reduced to doing mop-up work here and there when the Royals had big leads late or when they were so far behind that they were not likely to catch up. It was a far cry from his first ten or so years in the League, when his ERA was around 2.0 and better than most relievers in the game.

When Joe's father, Walter, found out that a segment of our vacation would take us through Kansas City and that the Royals would be in town while we were there, he called Joe and asked that he give the Neuhaus family the so-called 'Royal treatment' when we visited. Joe was happy to do so, and to this day, it remains one of the most memorable experiences of childhood for both Greg and me.

Walter gave Dad Joe's phone number and told us to call him at his Kansas City home around noon on the day of the seven p.m. game we would be attending against the Minnesota Twins. My dad called, as instructed, and sure enough, Joe answered and told us what to do. The plan was to meet him at the press gate of the new Royals stadium at three p.m., long before anyone was at the park, and he would gives us a VIP Tour. Joe did not disappoint.

Right at three, as promised, Joe was at the press gate and seemed genuine in his delight in meeting his hometown fans. He took us on a tour of the press boxes and media dining room and also down into the Royals locker room, where I was shocked to see there was a keg of Falstaff beer on tap. We came up out of the locker room into the dugout and got to sit on the benches and peer out over the pristine field from the exact place the Major Leaguers would be doing so a few short hours later.

Then Joe asked Greg and me a question that took all of one second for us to answer: "Would you boys like to run the bases?" *Did he really just ask us that?* We were up over the rail of the dugout instantly, headed to first base as fast as our legs would carry us. We rounded the bags, touching the inside corners with our foot, just as we had been taught in Little League, and then the big finale: the slide into home plate as we completed the round. Wow! It was the absolute coolest thing we had done to date in our young lives, completely unbelievable and surreal, like something out of a boy's sweetest dreams.

Just as Greg and I were preparing to ask Joe if we could do it again, a player and a coach, both in gym shorts and t-shirts, came out to the infield. The coach began to hit ground balls to the player, who fielded them, and then dropped them in a five-gallon plastic bucket placed next to third base. We thought it was odd for them to be there, as not another soul was in the stadium. Joe asked Greg and me if we would like to get the player's autograph. More out of a sense of politeness than anything, since we didn't recognize him, we said we would love to have his autograph, though it really wasn't true. After all, if the guy had to come out early and take extra practice before anyone else, and the first baseman was not even there to catch his throw, clearly he was no one of importance, and his autograph would just be worthless scribble. Still, not wanting Joe to think we were ungrateful, Greg and I both approached the scrub player with one of the dated game-day programs Joe had given each of us. We asked for his autograph, pretending to sound enthusiastic. Of course he was glad to oblige, since we were surely the only people who would ever ask him. We figured we were doing him a favor, giving him a chance to feel flattered like the good players, whose autographs we really wanted—people like Amos Otis, Cookie Rojas, John Mayberry, Bob Tewkesbury, Luis Aparicio, and the other famous players coming to the field. A few other players began to arrive and stretch and prepare for batting practice, so Joe suggested we take our seats next to the on-deck circle right beside the Royals dugout. He promised that later, he would send all the players over that we wanted autographs from, and again, he did not disappoint.

While we were waiting for the good players' autographs, I told Greg to discretely dispose of the tainted program with the unwanted autograph, and we would get all of the good ones on the other clean and unblemished one. Greg took one last look at the scribbled signature, which neither one of us could interpret. Just before he proceeded to crumple the unwanted program, he said, "Yeah, it looks like this guy's first name is George." If we needed any other evidence of why the program should be tossed, that was it. We had never heard of a person by the name of George who was the least bit cool. In fact, the only George we had ever known was Steve and John Lyness's stepdad, and we thought he was quite a loser. Cookie, Louis, and Amos were cool names. Thus, the dated program, with Future Hall of Fame third baseman George Brett's rookie autograph on it, personalized to Roger and Greg, was discarded under our seat and left for the custodians to sweep away after the game. Seemed like a good idea at the time, but hindsight is twenty-twenty.

CHAPTER 28

Uncle Who?

In addition to Uncle Donnie, the only other of my father's brothers to whom we were very connected was Uncle Billy, as we knew him. Later in life, we would hear other adults refer to him as Gerald, Gerry, and Bean, and we eventually discovered his real name was Gerald, but he was always Uncle Billy to us. I am not sure where the name came from, as it was a bit odd, but the mystery remains unexplained to this day.

Billy was many things. He was a fireman, a contractor, an independent business owner, a foster parent, and the inventor of a couple of household products that never really caught on. But perhaps above all else, Uncle Billy was a real bull shitter. He was a verbal antagonist who was really good at drawing my Dad into heated debates. One of the classics they engaged in occurred in June of 1972, the night my oldest sister M.L. and Billy's oldest son, our cousin, Michael, graduated from high school.

In the summer of '72, the controversy surrounding the Vietnam War continued to be a point of contention and tension among Americans. Many of the battle lines here at home seemed to be drawn across generational lines. Young people in their teens and early twenties were largely against the war and were aggressive in exercising their Constitutional rights to freedom of speech and public assembly as means for expressing their dissent and disapproval. One such fellow, Ben Vernon, a member of M.L. and Michael's graduating class at Dubuque Senior High School, found a medium for exercising his rights by parading across stage at the 1972 commencement with a bright red peace symbol and the words 'Peace Now!' stitched across the front of his gown.

Just as it did at the ceremony, Ben's statement became a topic of conversation and controversy during the post-ceremonial celebration our families held for M.L. and Michael at 116 later that evening.

Dad and Uncle Bill were sipping on a few Coke Highs, which consisted of Jim Beam whiskey and Coca-Cola on the rocks. As the drinks went down, the conversation became more intense. Dad went on and on about how Ben should not have been allowed to wear his message on his gown and hat, saying it was disgraceful and disrespectful and was a distraction from the true purpose of the ceremony, which was to honor the graduates. Even though Billy likely saw some merit to my dad's assertion, what fun would it have been for him to agree? So, Billy responded to my dad in counterpoint fashion with his own assertion that the boy was within his legal rights, and the only way we were ever going to end the war was if people spoke out against it in every forum available to them. The back-and-forth continued with shouting and cutting one another off, then trying to shout over one another. Every once in a while, Uncle Billy would interject something particularly provocative to my dad, then turn quickly over his shoulder with a devilish smile and wink toward those of us who had begun to gather around the table, much as we would on the playground at Nativity School when a fight was about to break out.

The debate festered to the point where Dad said Ben should have been thrown in jail, and Billy retorted by claiming he should have been given a medal of honor. At that point, my dad jumped from his chair with his finger pointed at Billy and began to close in on my uncle's personal space. Both men's faces were now red, and there was fire in their eyes.

Just then, the kitchen door opened, and who appeared but the man of the hour, Ben Vernon. "Hey, man! What's going on? ya gotta keep the peace in here, Daddies. Don't be sockin' it to each other. Ya gotta put a little love in your hearts."

At that, Dad and Billy were defused, and they both suddenly saw great humor in the fact that Ben was trying to make peace between them, having not a clue that his earlier antics were what had nearly brought them to blows. Peace now, Daddies! And with that, there was a ceasefire at 116.

CHAPTER 29

Good Knight, Bad Knight

The mixing of a few drinks, combined with his propensity for not being able to keep a zipper on his lips, got Uncle Billy into more than a few dilemmas that some might characterize as having seemed like good ideas at the time. One such occasion occurred at the Knights of Columbus (KC) Hall, and it became a full family effort to bail Uncle Bill out.

As my dad explained the inception of the events, it went something like this: One Tuesday evening, which happened to be the night of the monthly business meeting for the club, the KC hall was filled with members more interested in fun than anything else. But there was business to be done before the poker and euchre and bowling could get underway. Yes, the KC Hall had its own four-lane bowling alley on the downstairs level by the bar. It was late April, just four months before early August, when the Annual Dubuque County Fair would take place—a really big event for the KCs and the entire area. The fair was big for the KCs because they sold food and beverages from eleven a.m. to midnight for all seven days of the fair. The KC membership and a cadre of enlisted volunteers staffed the booth. I'm not sure how much of the club's annual treasury was dependent on the productivity of fair week, but I imagine those fair soft drinks and hot dogs accounted for a large percentage of whatever funds they raised.

Apparently, when it came to the item on the meeting agenda where the election of a committee chairman to take responsibility for operation of the KC booth at the fair was discussed, there were no volunteers. The job was a big responsibility and required weeks of preparation before the fair even started. It included recruiting 200 or more volunteers, ordering all of the food, making bank deposits, and oversight of the booth during fair week, representing a total time commitment of probably 800 hours or more. The room was silent for some time with no takers, until one unknowingly emerged from the back of the room. "Oh c'mon," said Uncle Billy to the group, more interested in getting on with a good game of euchre than anything else. "This booth thing is not that big a deal. Somebody just agree to it so we can get on with tonight's festivities."

Bud Isenhart (the father of Chasman, the submarine-style pitcher) blurted out, "If you think it's so easy, then why don't you do it, Neuhaus?"

"Fine. I'll do it," said Billy.

The Grand Knight sat at the head table and asked, "All in favor?"

With the deal done, Gerald Neuhaus was appointed Chairman of the KC Booth for the 1975 Dubuque County Fair. And he had not a clue what he was in for or how he was going to do it, but the long-awaited euchre game was underway, and Billy was fine with that.

The next day, realizing the magnitude of his most recent error in judgment, Billy began to assess all that would need to be done and quickly became overwhelmed. He called Dad for help. The next thing we knew, all Neuhaus children over the age of twelve were told to make no plans for early August. Our week would be occupied assisting with the bailout of Uncle Billy in his role as Chairman of the KC Booth.

When Fair Week rolled around, I found myself responsible for a number of duties. Among them were selling RC Cola as a vendor in the grandstand during the evening headliner show and at the Sunday night stock car races, tractor pull and demolition derby. I also worked at the booth on the food line, preparing hot dogs, hamburgers, and French fries for the thousands of fair-goers while my mom and sisters toiled away in the back kitchen. My favorite and most fruitful role was working as cashier on the register at the end of the food line. Suddenly, the KC booth was a good place to work.

For obvious reasons, they usually tried to have adult volunteers handle cash register duties. But as the week wore on, after more and more adults had put in the shift or two they had committed to and were off the hook, there became a need for younger cashiers. Fortunately, I was there for my Uncle Billy and the Knights of Columbus. Ching! Ching!

I had spent in the neighborhood of thirty to forty hours volunteering at the booth in the early part of the week and had received no pay other than a few gratis hamburgers here and there. My hourly rate, however, was about to rise like tech stocks in the 1990's. Polka Dots was going to have to put an addition onto Hell to make room for not only me, but a number of my soon-to-be KC booth customer-friends. That is, if confession didn't do the trick.

Simply reaching into the cash register and peeling off dollars intended for the KC treasury seemed a bit too crass for a decent Catholic boy like me. I wondered one night as I was going to sleep and pondering my eleven-to-two shift at the register the next day, how I could operate my self-sanctioned bonus compensation plan. As I drifted off, the pieces fell into place. Before I headed to the fair the next morning, I called Carl Wisco. Carl was a guy I had just met that summer and would be attending high school with in the fall. He was the perfect accomplice because he knew no one at the KC booth, nor did any of them know him. This had to be a tight-lipped operation. Unlike the Search for Tomorrow, I would not even tell my much-trusted brother Tom, who was also working at the booth. That would have been too close for comfort on a heist of this magnitude.

Carl appeared at the booth as instructed during the lunch rush hour, when all the workers were busy and no one had time to be too observant of anything other than their own job. Carl slid his tray down the counter until he reached the cash register where I was working. When our eyes met, we engaged informally, as strangers do.

"A burger, fries, and a Coke. Will that be it, sir?" I asked.

"That's all," muttered my co-conspirator.

"That'll be three even," I said.

He passed me a five-dollar bill.

I took his five and changed it in the register, pulling out two bills to return to him: a one-dollar bill on top, and a twenty-dollar bill hidden underneath. "Two bucks is your change. Please visit the KC booth again and bring your friends," I said.

Carl wandered away, and I went on to the next customer.

As instructed, Carl did bring friends. Our scam worked to perfection, but we did not want to overdo it, so he sent three different guys to me in the next day and returned once himself. Each time, the KC dollar exchange rate continued to be favorable as compared to rate of the currency they passed me. All proceeds were split 50/50. If anyone were to ask me about volunteering at the KC booth, I would tell them, "It's good work if you can get it." I was beginning to hope Uncle Billy would volunteer to be chairman again the following year, but there was no such luck. He had learned his lesson, so my gig was up . . . but at least I always had house painting to fall back on.

CHAPTER 30

Cousin Kevin to the Rescue

Another fond memory that relates to my uncle Gerald, Gerry, Bean, Billy, or whatever the name *du jour* was, had to do with his middle son, and one of my favorite cousins, Kevin Neuhaus.

Kevin was just a year younger than my tyrant older brother Ken, five years older than me. Kevin was considerably more muscular and overall more physically developed than Ken. I learned early in life that if I treated my cousin well and could get him to take a liking to me, he could serve as a protector, a buffer between my brother and me. It worked like a charm. Whenever Kevin came over, I sucked up to him like he was the President-elect. I shared my bicycle with him, bought sodas and candy from Frank and John's for him, pointed out the cuter older neighborhood girls to him, and did whatever I thought might curry his favor.

One summer, Aunt Phyllis, (Uncle Billy's wife and Kevin's mother) was admitted to the University of Iowa Hospital in Iowa City for back surgery. Iowa City was about ninety miles from Dubuque, and Aunt Phyllis and Uncle Billy were going to have to stay for about two weeks while she underwent the surgery and first phase of rehabilitation. They had four children they needed help with during this time, so the four Neuhaus cousins were shopped out, one each, to live with four different Aunts and Uncles until Billy and Phyllis returned to Dubuque. As luck would have it, Kevin became our guest, and I could think of nothing cooler. I knew I would have to put up with nothing from my brother Ken for almost two weeks, as long as I could keep Kevin on my side, and that is exactly what I did. I stuck to Kevin like a bee to honey. I followed him around, laid out a sleeping bag for him alongside my bed, and gave him my best goose down feather pillow. Anytime Ken tried to mess with me or order me around, as he was prone to do, Kevin came to my rescue. The two came to blows several times the first week of our time together, almost always because Kevin was intervening on my behalf. Finally, Ken threw in the towel and resigned himself to the fact that I was on a free pass until Kevin went home. It was two truly great weeks for me.

During the second week of cousin Kevin's tenure as our adopted fifth brother, which just so happened to coincide with Fourth of July weekend, about a dozen of the neighborhood gang made the seven-block bicycle ride down Hill Street to a penny candy place called The Hillside Confectionary, which for some reason or other, we all called Babe's Candy Store—the Uncle Billy illogical naming principle at work again. This particular day, Kevin's strong and ample calves powered my bicycle while I rode on the handlebars. We loved to go to Babe's because it was the prototypical kid-in-a-candy-store fantasy shop. Although Frank and John had all kinds of candy in their gas station racks, Babe's massive wood and glass cases were immeasurably better. Everything Frank and John's sold, you could buy at a multitude of grocery stores and gas stations. Babe's, on the other hand, was the purveyor of the most unique kinds of items one could imagine, things that could not be found anywhere else.

The moment we pushed open the full-view glass hydraulic-hinged door, with the metal hand bar that stretched across the middle, a distinct aroma greeted us. In a word, it was sweet. As we set foot inside, the yellow pine hardwood floor squeaked with every step we took. The first aisle on the left was lined on both sides with penny and five-cent candy and a variety of small toys and novelties, proudly displayed right at eye level for the consumer set twelve years and under, clearly the target market at Babe's. There were multi-colored and flavored bubble gum cigars; candy cigarettes with red tips on the ends to suggest they were lit; Slo Poke chocolate-covered caramel suckers; candy necklaces and bracelets of round candies strung on just enough elastic to fit snuggly around a child's neck or wrist; Razzles, a kind of hard candy that turned to chewing gum when you bit into it; Bub's Daddy bubble gum sticks about the diameter of a pencil and ten to twelve inches in length; malted milk balls; colorful Candy Buttons, tiny bits of hard candy that were adhered to a piece of paper in neat little tasty rows; Ring Pops suckers, like candy pacifiers that we could put on our fingers and suck on at our leisure throughout the day; Sweet Tarts; Sugar Babies; watermelon Jujus; Whistle Pops we could blow on until the temptation to bite into them ended the tune; Jolly Ranchers; orange-flavored candy wax harmonicas we could play until we had to give in to the desire to experience the chewy texture; Milk Duds; and so much more. The choices were limitless . . . and that was just the candy section. The freezer section was equally overwhelming with more dairy choices than Phelper could shake a stick at. There were orange sherbet Push Ups, the cylindrical treat that could be pushed up from the bottom out of its mold and into your mouth; Mr. Freeze pops; Bomb Pops; frozen Hires Root Beer pops with vanilla ice cream centers; ice cream sandwiches; Drumsticks; miniature ice cream sundaes in shallow plastic cups that came completely accessorized with a small wooden spoon; and many other delicious frozen delights.

On the day we went there with our cousin Kevin around the Fourth of July, though, it was about all things sulfur. On the back wall at Babe's, there were no food items, but rather toys, trinkets, and red-white-and-blue novelties ordered specially for the Independence Day celebration: sparklers, cap guns, smoking snakes, cork and string-loaded parachute troopers, and our all-time favorite, smoke bombs.

Smoke bombs resembled miniature cannonballs. They were round that way, but only about the size of a large grape, with a fuse that protruded about one inch out the top. When the fuse was lit and burned into the center of the orb, a poignant, sulfur-smelling stench emitted smoke that would be consistent with the outside color of the bomb, leaving a nasty stain on skin, clothing, the sidewalk, or anything else the vapors came into contact with. Smoke bombs were a cheap thrill: one for a nickel or three for ten cents. Amongst our neighborhood crew that day, we probably bought about fifty of them, and we were back on the bikes, up Hill Street and over to Langworthy Avenue to an open, park-like green area that was enclosed on the perimeter by apple trees and consumed about two-thirds of a city block. We called the space The Apple Orchard, and it was a frequent location for many of our neighborhood escapades.

We played a series of team-oriented smoke bomb games in The Apple Orchard all afternoon. There were about four or five guys per team. Essentially, two teams hid amongst the bushes, trees, and wooded areas in the orchard, while the third team closed their eyes and counted to 100. Upon reaching the count of 100, the third team would embark on a hunt in which each team member could toss one of his lit smoke bombs into a hidden area in hopes of flushing out one of the hidden teams we guessed might be in that area. We rotated being the hunter and the hunted for several hours until my sister M.L. was sent up the block, at the request of my mom, to find us and let us know it was time to come home for dinner. When M.L. located us, we had four smoke bombs remaining but no time to use them, so Ken slipped them all in his pocket, and we headed home to get ready for dinner.

Upon arriving back at 116, Ken, Tom, Kevin, and I washed up for dinner, taking turns using the single bathroom sink that was shared by all eleven members of the household. (We also had just one phone, as did most homes back then.) After getting properly scrubbed up and now ready to satisfy our hearty appetites, we were informed that my dad would be a little late coming home from work, so dinner would be a bit delayed. We wandered down to the basement to amuse ourselves for a few minutes while we waited.

As we searched for ways to entertain ourselves, Ken was struck with one of his brilliant ideas. "Hey guys," he said, "let's finish off these smoke bombs."

"Are you nuts?" replied Tom, playing his usual voice of reason role with Ken. "Those things reek. Mom will even smell them upstairs. Besides," he continued, "the colored smoke will stain the floor and ceiling down here."

"No problem," replied Ken, overcoming the objection, which he was always quick to do. "We'll just open a window."

The basement windows at 116 were about two feet long and eighteen inches high, and there were only two of them. Ken told Kevin to prop one open, which he did, at which time Ken torched the fuse of a bright yellow smoke bomb. The spew of stench and color filled the entire downstairs in record time, as Tom made a beeline across the room to prop open the other window.

Our little game was spiraling out of control in a rapid fashion. The four of us were coughing and trying to fan the mustard-colored haze out the two windows with pieces of cardboard we had torn off of boxes Mary had brought home from the Warehouse Market, and then we heard it: the door opening at the top of the basement stairs, followed by heavy footsteps descending upon us stair by stair. We didn't need to see who was coming through the smoke, as we already knew by the thunderous footsteps and eerie silence. It was Big Kenny, our father, ready to issue royal ass kicking all around. Even Kevin couldn't save us from Dad's wrath. For some reason, it occurred to me that it must be time for dinner. After all, Dad was home. I even thought for a brief moment that somehow we could blame him for the stinky yellow hue in our basement, because if he had come home from work on time, we would have been at the dinner table and not in the basement getting into mischief. On second thought, I realized it might be best not to share that reasoning.

"What the hell is going on down here?!" Dad shouted as his intimidating frame came into view and more into focus after crossing through the fog the bomb had left lingering, now mostly confined to the ceiling rafters of the basement. He lined the four of us up against the limestone block walls of the basement, like soon-to be victims of a firing squad. Is he even going to give us blindfolds? I wondered. As Big Ken lectured us on the ignorance of the act and the fire safety issues we had breached, he reached into young Ken's pocket and yanked out the remaining bombs, pulling the fuses from each one, then grinding them into the damp concrete basement floor with the weathered black shoes he wore to work on the loading dock at Torbert Drug. As Dad began to threaten sending Kevin to another cousin's house for the remainder of the time his parents would be in Iowa City and we all pleaded that we be given a second chance, our pleas were drowned out by the sound of a fire engine. Joe Rand, our neighbor across Solon Street had called the fire department when he observed smoke billowing from the basement window some minutes earlier. He was sure 116 was about to burn to the ground, and really, who could blame him? After Big Ken endured the embarrassment of having to go out and explain to the firemen the real source of the smoke and apologize for the faux tragedy and waste of their time, he returned to the house even more upset than before. He ordered all of us upstairs to the bedroom we shared and administered a heaping helping of some not-so-good, but definitely old-fashioned discipline.

We were denied dinner that evening and confined to our room for the rest of the night. We slept on our stomachs, considering our backsides were much too tender.

CHAPTER 31

School Friends

In our days of youth, we really had two distinct sets of friends. There were the neighborhood friends, and there were the school friends. Although there were lots of kids who lived in our neighborhood, many of us attended different schools—St. Joseph's, Washington, and Lincoln in addition to Nativity, so we all had a second set of friends from the schools we attended. Surprisingly, there was little crossover between the neighborhood friends and school friends.

At Nativity, my main group of friends included Jimmy 'Kinger' King, Steve 'Kipper' Kane, Jay 'Jungo' Jungblut, Ken 'Beanie' Botsford, Tom 'Pie Man' Crimmins, and Jeff 'Shleets' Schlueter. The lone neighborhood friend who doubled as a school friend was Tom 'Hot Dog' Schute (the Root Beer Chemist). And then there were the girls for whose interest and fancy we all competed: Julie Hoffmann, Lisa Kingsley, Nancy Gearhardt, Annie and Marty McKay, Nita Frommelt, and Mary Kuehnle, among others.

As referenced previously, Nativity School was the Catholic school of choice for the Neuhaus family, even though St. Joseph's was a little closer. All of my parents' children attended Nativity for grades one through eight. We were taught virtually all subjects by nuns who were members of the Order of the Sisters of the Visitation. Some were so old they had even taught my mother at the Academy of the Visitation, located across Alta Vista from Nativity. The Viz Convent adjoined the girls' high school. The subjects we studied included reading, writing, and arithmetic, along with social studies, music, and lots of religion. I don't recall there being any lay (non-priest or nun) teachers at Nativity until around the time I entered the sixth grade. Nativity Church stood immediately north of the school, and together, the parish structures occupied an entire city-sized block, a compound when you included the Viz campus across the street, and Loras College, a 65 acre campus just one block west. Nearly all of my school friends lived near the immediate area of the compound, a few blocks to the north and west, which bordered the Loras campus, a Catholic college (all male until 1971) operated by the Archdiocese of Dubuque. If we were a gang, this combined area would have been considered our turf. Every kid within a five—or six-block area was a Nativity Royal. The Nativity and Loras campuses were our stomping grounds and provided us with the basis for many adventurous evening and weekend activities from September through the end of May.

When I was in the seventh grade, as result of my close neighborhood relationship to Tom Schute, a popular eighth grader, I spent a fair amount of time in the company of Royals who were a year older than me. The older boys included Dave Mettille, Jim Spears, and Kevin Donovan. While it was a privilege to hang with these guys because it provided access to groups of eighth-grade girls who otherwise would never have even talked to me, as well as crossover socialization with cool kids from other Catholic schools like St. Anthony's and Holy Ghost, there was a price to be paid for being the junior partner, so to speak.

I recall one evening in the spring of 1974. I was a seventh grader accompanying my eighth-grade mentors on a foot trek a good three miles or so to the home of Beth Helling, one of the most attractive girls from St. Anthony's School. The Hellings had a cool house that bordered Flora Park. They had a huge back yard with a trampoline in it and a furnished walk-in basement/recreation room with ping-pong, foosball, and a pool table. It was a popular hangout for a mix of several schools' social elite. When I was so lucky to be invited along, it typically meant I would be the youngest at the gathering. As we walked across the neighborhoods, several of us wearing Nativity football jerseys we had stolen from the school equipment room over the course of the winter, my underling status was called upon by Dave Mettille, who had a thing for Lori Menadue, one of the prime St. Anthony girls. Lori lived between Nativity and the Hellings' house, so Dave told Lori we would stop by her place on our walk to Beth's that evening and escort her to the get-together. Lori was to be prepared for the doorbell to ring promptly at six thirty p.m. and bid her parents farewell for the night, claiming a girlfriend was meeting her to walk over to the Helling's.

When we reached the Menadue residence on Atlantic Street, none of us really wanted to be the one to ring the doorbell and wait for Lori, because we all perceived her dad to be a rather intimidating figure and had no interest in a chance meeting with him. Although we all knew she was Mettille's girl, and it should be his duty to knock on the door, rank was pulled on me, and I was designated to call for Lori while Schute, Mettille, Spears, and Donovan hid behind the bushes that lined the sidewalk in front of the home. As I crept quietly up the walk, peering through the picture window that exposed the family room, I could see the TV was on. I could see the back of Mr. and Mrs. Menadue's heads as they viewed an episode of *The Partridge Family.* My elder friends had assured me Lori was on cue and would respond to the door before her parents would have a chance to get up, so it was an unsettling surprise when my knuckles hit the door. The first person up and out of his chair was none other than Charlie Menadue. Through the window, I could see him approaching to respond to my inquiry. At that point, I went into frozen, shock-like terror, going completely blank and dumbstruck, as I hadn't rehearsed a speech to explain my presence at the doorstep. There was no way I could tell the man I was there to pick up his daughter, who was supposed to be the one answering the door. Fear ruled the moment, and visions of immediate possible exit strategies raced around my spinning head.

When Mr. Menadue opened the door, looking down upon me authoritatively from the top step, I became paralyzed. "Yes?" Charlie inquired, as he looked at me with a questioning stare.

"Is this the Menadue residence?" I quipped.

"It most certainly is," he replied.

"Oh. I'm so sorry," I blurted out apologetically. "I must have the wrong house. Goodnight."

I turned away from the house, shuffling down the five or six cement stairs before breaking into a jog upon reaching the sidewalk. My accomplices were already about two blocks ahead of me, making their escape. Just like that, we were gone, and Lori Menadue was on her own if she was going to the Hellings that night. It was an early lesson learned about waiting on women, and one I wouldn't soon forget. Thank God Mr. Menadue let me live to tell the tale.

CHAPTER 32

Kipper, by George

Of all the Nativity gang, Kipper Kane was easily the most intriguing and unique. The 1972 Olympics were held in Munich, Germany and will forever be remembered for the tragic invasion of the Israeli team camp by Arab terrorists. Less remembered about those games was a marathon runner from a tiny village in Kenya who trained by running in his bare feet up and down the rugged mountain terrain near his Third World home. That determined runner's name was Kip Cano (K-no), and that was how Kipper's nickname originated.

Like Kip Cano, Kipper Kane marched to the beat of his own drum. He was fearless, street smart, daring, a wise cracker, and completely unthreatened by authority, including the nuns at Nativity School. One other thing about Kipper was that he had a vast vocabulary. He knew more forbidden words as a kid than all of the grown men at Frank and John's Gulf Station combined.

Kipper had an older brother by the name of Mike, who was the same age as my brother Tom. As a result, for two years, when Kip and I were in fifth and sixth grades, and our brothers were in the seventh and eighth grade, the four of us would sometimes run together—not run as in Kip Cano, but as in hanging out.

One Saturday morning, as we often did in the winter, the four of us met at the Keyline bus stop in front of the apartment where the Kanes lived and, for a dime, rode the bus downtown to Fisher Bowling Lanes. At Fisher Lanes, we could bowl two games, rent our shoes, and have a cherry Coke (the kind with added cherry syrup)—all for a buck.

One of the things that set Kipper apart from the rest of us was his ability to fearlessly impersonate and mimic adults in ways they were not sure how to interpret. One such person Kipper loved to do this to was George Henson, the manager of Fisher Lanes. If George had not been in the business of managing Fisher Lanes, there may have been a place for him on the crew at Frank and John's. He was about five-foot-eight, weighed about 200 pounds, and always wore the same navy slacks with a white pullover knit shirt, that scarcely covered his protruding basketball-sized gut. His first name was even embroidered over the breast pocket in cursive writing, and his shirt was never tucked in. George wore black horn-rimmed glasses with Coke-bottle lenses.

If there was a problem with any of the lanes, a press of the red CALL button would ring a bell at the shoe rental counter, where George casually sat on a barstool, leaning against the counter, chewing and sucking on a half-lit White Owl blunt cigar. The buttons were only supposed to be pressed if there was an actual problem, but Kipper loved to use it just to yank George's chain.

On this particular day, Kip pressed the button, and we could see George jump as the *buzz* at the counter interrupted his daydream. Off and walking at a brisk pace came George toward our lane to see what the problem was. Mike, Tom, and I had no idea what Kipper was going to do, but knowing what he was capable of, we were getting worried. As George approached, Kip turned his back to us. When George arrived at our lane, Kip turned slowly around. He had our scoring pencil hanging out of the corner of his mouth and was chewing on it the way George was infamous for chewing his cigars. Kipper had tucked his bowling ball up under his shirt, simulating George's potbelly. He had one hand under the shirt, supporting the weight of the ball, and the other on the outside, rubbing around on it the way George would scratch on his own rotund middle. When George asked what the problem was, we all looked at Kipper to respond. He looked to George and exclaimed, "I can't find my ball. I know it's here somewhere, but I just sat it down on the return to score my last frame, and it disappeared. Have you seen it anywhere?"

As George began to examine which balls were on the return, Kipper walked around behind him, mimicking his every move. "What did it look like?" George asked, trying to be accommodating to his paying customers.

"It's black, round, weighs about ten pounds, and answers to the name of Skippy," replied Kipper.

As George turned slowly around with a black ten-pound ball from the return, Kipper followed in his footsteps behind his back and slid the other ball out from under his shirt and down onto the return. As George turned back around and bumped into Kipper with the ball, Kip stretched out his arms to receive the other ball and shouted out "George, you found Skippy! You found Skippy! How can I ever repay you?"

George looked mystified as he glanced over at the other three of us, then back at Kipper, as if to say "What the hell is wrong with your whacked-out buddy?" George waddled back to the counter as we all tried to muffle our hysterical laughter until he would no longer be able to hear us.

It was vintage Kipper Kane, an irreverent action taken simply because it was at the expense of someone else. We thought it was terrible and somewhat rude to George, but we could not resist laughing . . . and obviously, it was a memorable occasion.

Kipper had another talent that was downright freaky. He could peel the top of his eyelids back up into his head and kind of tuck them under the upper part of his eye socket, exposing the inner pink and tissue that covers the eye when you blink. Kipper would get on the bus, spot an elderly woman with a shopping bag and an open seat next to her, and he would zone in. He would walk toward the open seat, turn his back to the woman, flip his eyelids up, and then turn back around, sitting down quickly, stretching his face out close to hers as he invaded her space. He insisted on saying something to get her attention, like, "Is this seat taken?" or "Do you mind if I sit here?" Then he would go into some made-up story about being on the way to the eye doctor for his annual exam when his eyelids flipped up and he could not get them back down. He took things even further by imploring the old lady to show him what she had in her bag and put the finishing touches on his prank by asking if she would tug on his eyelids a little to help him get them back to where they were supposed to be. It was an absolute circus to watch. We just could not help ourselves, or Kipper, for that matter . . . and Lord knows that boy needed help!

CHAPTER 33

First Taste

I can vividly remember my first experience with alcohol. It was in the company of Kip and Kinger.

James Leo King was the fourth of five children born to Leo and Janaan King. During the school years from fifth through eighth grade, I think I spent more time at the King residence on Melrose Terrace than I did at 116; in fact, I'm sure of it. Kingers' house was only about three blocks away from 116, but it was in a direction that somehow crossed summer/school year buddy lines, so we did not see each other from June until the end of August but were inseparable for the entire school years that spanned 1972 through 1975. Summers, for both of us, were reserved for the neighborhood kids.

Kinger idolized his much older brother David. They were separated by about eight years in age, so it was as though they skipped all the issues Ken and I had dealt with earlier in life, being more contemporaries, and fast forwarded right to the part where David was just a cool guy we all looked up to. David (who everyone called 'Wally' because he chose to button the top button on his high school letterman jacket, and they thought it made him look like a walrus) stood about six-six. To us, he seemed more like a giant than a walrus. David was a pretty good basketball player—good enough, at least, to play at the next level when he went off to school at St. Mary's University in Winona, Minnesota, about 200 miles north of Dubuque.

It was November of 1972, and I was in the sixth grade. David King was in his sophomore year at St. Mary's, and Mr. and Mrs. King took Janie, Jimmy's little sister, to Winona with them to attend the opening of Wally's basketball season and Parents' Weekend. Jimmy was entrusted to the care of his two older sisters. Kathy had just started college, and Laura was in her last year at Wahlert. It was a big error in judgment by Leo and Janaan, as they would have been better off leaving Kinger, Kipper, and me home alone.

Saturday night arrived. Kathy King was interim head of the Melrose Terrace household and self-appointed hostess to the biggest weekend beer bash known to the in crowd at Wahlert High School. She told Kinger he could invite two friends over, but they had to be able to keep a secret. Kip and I were the obvious candidates, and Kathy and Laura knew us well. They pretty much treated us like two younger brothers, so it was a natural groove for all of us.

When I arrived at Kingers front door, the outside scene was that of a crisp autumn darkness. The smell of burning leaves was omnipresent, as was the cool temperature that showed up like clockwork that time of year and sent a chill down the front of my unzipped hooded sweatshirt. This was a high school party, and I knew it would be completely uncool to zip up my sweatshirt.

There were an unusual number of cars, unfamiliar to the neighborhood, lining both sides of the typically quiet street, and Kingers' driveway, which typically might have one car parked in it, if any, looked something akin to a used car lot in need of an inventory reduction blowout sale. There must have been at least a dozen vehicles parked every which way, some with tires that encroached on the grass that lined the concrete drive. Leo would not have approved, but the driveway was the least of the evils Leo would have been displeased with that night.

I must be late, I thought. I was a bit nervous and unsure of what to expect. I always just walked into Kingers' house like it was my own, but on this strangely different night, somehow I felt compelled to ring the bell. I rang the doorbell four times, and no one answered. There was a lot of noise going on inside, and I considered opening the door and inviting myself in when three high school kids emerged from a briefly stopped passing car that continued down Melrose Terrace after its drive-by drop-off. Each of the three partygoers carried a brown paper grocery bag with their arms wrapped around it to hold it waist high. There was some weight to their mystery cargo for sure, and as they came up the stairs and on to the Victorian-style wraparound wooden porch, one of them asked if I could please open the door to the house and hold it while they entered with the supplies.

I obliged the request for assistance. As I stood holding the door, the last guy through reached into his bag with one hand and plucked out a quart bottle of Falstaff beer by its neck and swung it my way. "Thanks, kid," he said, and they disappeared into the crowd assembled inside the living room.

I followed them inside and found myself standing amongst a lot of drunken people I did not know, holding a quart of beer that I really had no idea what to do with. As I gazed around the room, seeking to locate Kinger and Kipper, the obvious answer came to me: I should unscrew the aluminum cap, throw back a swig, and act like I know what I'm doing. It seemed to work, and I made quick work of that quart and followed shortly with another. The bitter taste of the hops and the burn of the carbonation as the cold liquid journeyed down my throat manifested itself as a full feeling in my stomach. At that moment, more of a reflex than a premeditated action, I let out a hefty belch, which gave my stomach immediate relief. I realized in that moment how amazing nature and the human body's ability to adapt is. I now had room for another swig, and it was getting easier. After a few healthy swigs from the second quart, I decided it was time to go find Kip and Kinger and show them what I had learned.

I navigated my way around the house, bumping, being bumped, spilling and being spilled upon, in search of my buddies. Not finding them on the main level of the house, I ventured upstairs to investigate the game room and bedroom areas. All of the bedroom doors were closed, and each had a group of three or four couples hovering around the outside, appearing to be waiting for something. I thought they must be waiting to use the bathroom, but when that door opened and the person who had been in there left, no one seemed to be in a hurry to occupy it.

The minute a bedroom door opened, however, several couples seemed to be in a hurry to stake claim to the vacancy. I began to realize what was going on and quickly decided this was not a place I should be.

Just then, another bedroom door opened, and a high school girl with a disgusted look on her face and an aggressive stomp to her walk exited the room, but no one seemed to want to go in there. Curiosity got the best of me, so I peered around the doorway and stuck my head in. There on the bed was a fellow by the name of Mike Berendes, wearing his Wahlert football jersey, and looking like he had just been laid out by the likes of Dick Butkus or some other NFL linebacker. He was pretty much semi-conscious, talking to himself in slurred fashion, with a quart bottle of Falstaff tucked under his arm like a teddy bear. Upon further review, it appeared he was attempting to make love to his bottle of brew, but whatever the case, I realized why the room was not in demand and concluded it would be wise to resume my search for Kip and Kinger downstairs.

When I reached the landing at the bottom of the stairs that entered the living room in one direction and the kitchen in the other, I decided to go the kitchen route this time. There, leaning up against the breakfast bar, were my long-lost compadres. We caught up with each other on the various things we had observed thus far in the young evening and agreed things were getting a bit out of hand, at least for saplings like ourselves. We took our bottles outside to the back steps near the basketball court. It was a familiar place we had utilized for hours every night during the spring, and there, where we felt most comfortable that night, we had our own little fest.

Saturday nights were great, but the one downside to them was that Sunday mornings always followed. For a sixth grader who managed a *Dubuque Telegraph-Herald* paper route, that meant a six a.m. wake-up call, followed by a good hour of delivering the morning newspaper . . . and Sunday was always the thickest, heaviest edition.

After downing about a quart and a half of Chicago White Sox announcer Harry Caray's favorite beer, I felt the need to head home and get some sleep before the dreaded Sunday morning alarm went off. The three-block walk/stumble from 1075 Melrose Terrace to 116 Nevada seemed to take forever. I was cold and drunk. The sidewalk kept moving on me as I treaded forward, swaying left to right with my head down. I tripped and fell several times. The strange thing was, it didn't even hurt when I hit the concrete sidewalk—not until the next morning, that is. I was out the moment my head hit the pillow that night. I had experienced my first taste of alcohol that evening, and it seemed like a pretty fun thing . . . at least that night.

CHAPTER 34

Paying the Price

The six o'clock alarm came early on Sunday morning. It seemed louder than normal, and unlike any other Sunday I could remember, it really made my head hurt a lot. I slapped at the clock on the nightstand near my bed, missing it several times before knocking it clear off the table and on the floor, where it seemed to die. A moment later, I believed death might be a better option than what I was experiencing. When I swung my feet over the side of the bed and onto the bedroom floor, I strangely already felt I needed to rest, even though I had just woke up. When I stood up straight, blood seemed to rush to my head, which was now throbbing. I felt dizzy as I began the agonizing walk down the hall toward the one bathroom on the main floor at 116. Suddenly, I felt sick to my stomach. The only time I could remember a similar feeling was when I had the flu. My first thought was that I had caught something from the people at the party. It was stuffy and crowded in the house, and I was sure there must have been a lot of germs spread amongst the guests. I felt saliva begin to gather in my mouth, enough to produce a drool. I rushed into the bathroom with a sense of urgency, dropped to my knees, and hung my head into the toilet, looking the water in the bowl eye to eye, and . . . nothing. I needed to puke, but it would not come up. It was bizarre. I was sick as a dog and still could not produce what was always produced when I had the flu. It was then that I was struck with the realization that it was only November, and the first confirmed cases of the influenza never arrived in Iowa until December at the earliest, some years not even until January. It took that long for me to begin to piece together the correlation between my activity from the previous night and my current state of health. As I stared into the toilet, wanting so badly to be done with this, I began with the plea that is known to anyone who ever drank too much for the first time. "Please, God . . . if you will just let me feel better right now, I will never drink again as long as I live. Cross my heart."

As I ventured out into the overcast, dark, damp morning at a drunken snail's pace, I pondered what had gone on the night before. There were things I could remember and things I could not. How did I get home? I wondered to myself. *Oh yeah!* My now aching knees, both of which were bruised and scratched, reminded me. They told me I had walked—or had at least attempted to walk. Drinking was not nearly as fun the day after, and I wondered how the same substance could cause two such dramatically different effects. It was baffling. I had drank too much and was paying the price in experiencing my first hangover, although I was still not even aware of the terminology. I had heard the term 'morning sickness' used in our house when my mom was pregnant with my youngest sibling Paula, and for a moment, I thought maybe this is what they were referring to. It was morning, and I was really sick, so that had to be it. I had morning sickness, that thing you get when you drink too much beer. I wondered if I would have to tell the priest about this at confession. I called Kip and Kinger later that day to compare notes. It made me feel a little better when I found both of them had morning sickness as well. My mom was puzzled when I was not hungry for lunch or dinner that day, and she asked me if I was feeling all right.

"Yes," I said. "I'm just not hungry."

She knew something was up, for I seldom turned down a meal, but I don't think it ever even came close to entering her mind that I was hung over. After all, what mother would suspect her sixth-grade son of having morning sickness?

CHAPTER 35

Bingo!

I entered the eighth grade at Nativity School in the autumn of 1974. Although my two oldest sisters attended a couple of years at the Academy of the Visitation, an all-girls high school also run by the same sisters that were in charge of Nativity School, Catholic high school would not be in my future.

'The Viz", as we called it, closed its academy doors in June 1970. The cost was getting to be prohibitive, younger nuns were leaving the order, and single-gender schools had begun to decline in popularity. Wahlert High School, named for a prominent Catholic Dubuque family that also operated the Dubuque Pack for several generations, became the transfer destination for about 99 percent of the girls from The Viz—but not M.L. and Patsy. With the high cost of private school tuition, combined with the reality of six more kids following them over the next eight years, the dollar signs lost out to the public school option as my parents examined family finances. Dubuque Senior High School, at a cost of about twenty-five dollars per year for books and fees, would become the destination for my two oldest sisters and the eventual *alma mater* for all the Neuhaus kids. I guess we were destined to be Rams, but not without a good effort first by the two girls, and the priests and nuns at Nativity to try and persuade and pressure our parents to have us attend Wahlert.

Because money was a considerable obstacle for many families when it came to choosing private schools over public schools, the parish leaders at Nativity implemented an eighth-grade grade student work program whereby all eighth graders who wanted to attend Wahlert Catholic the following year and needed financial assistance were offered jobs setting up and taking down the tables and chairs that transformed the school gymnasium into a bingo parlor every Monday night. For every hour a student committed to table and chair detail, the church would credit one dollar into a scholarship account to be applied against the cost of their freshman year at Wahlert. Of the twenty-five or so boys in my class, about twenty took advantage of this opportunity. Among those who did not were Kipper Kane and I. Despite the attempts of the Church to shame our parents and coerce us through peer pressure into going to Wahlert, we held out, but there were a handful of occasions when Kip and I ended up helping with table and chair detail anyway, and we profited handsomely in a way we liked much better than a lousy tuition fund.

Around 1970, as a way to aid churches in the state, the Iowa legislature made exceptions to the State laws that governed games of chance, and the sale of alcohol. Bingo was allowed one night per week, and beer could be sold during the bingo-playing hours. Games of chance were also allowed at the annual church festival. The Catholics got good at this quick. In fact, we even doubled down on both relaxed laws at once by allowing people to bet twenty-five cents per number on a spinning wheel for the chance to win a twelve-pack of beer. What a deal!

The Dubuque Star Brewery down by the train bridge where the tracks crossed the river from Illinois to Iowa brewed beer in an on again/off again fashion. They had success with one label, and then bombed with another, almost going out of business as a result. One beer that hit it big back in the 1970's was Pickett's Premium, named for the brew master at the time, Joe Pickett. As a result, Pickett's became the beer of choice at the Nativity Bingo Night, and it so happened that parish leaders stored the beer in the same room where the bingo tables and chairs were kept. It was the same room where Kip and I found the inspiration to conduct service to the parish through table and chair duty, never demanding a penny for a scholarship fund. That's just the kind of Good Samaritans that we were.

Few eighth graders in the Class of 1975 at Nativity School had ever been drunk in their young lives. The fear of God and going to Hell for doing bad things kept most of them away from such experimentation, unlike our "heathen" counterparts at the public schools, a number of whom had not only been drunk, but had also, based on gossip we had heard, smoked pot and cast their sexual purity to the wind long ago.

One Monday morning, Kip laid out a plan whereby the two of us would join with our Wahlert-bound classmates as volunteers, hauling the tables and chairs from the bingo storage room to the school gymnasium, but the tables and chairs weren't all Kip planned on hauling. He was intently focused on one of the twelve-packs of Pickett's Premium that were stacked about ten high and five across against the back wall of the cool, damp, dark storage room. When we exited the bingo storage room, below ground level of the Nativity Church, there was a bright hallway we called 'the tunnel'. The tunnel connected the school and church from below ground to allow the grade-school students to walk easily from class to Mass without going outside during the sub-zero winter months. A right turn into the tunnel when exiting the bingo storage room led to the school gymnasium, and a left turn led to the church. As a dozen or so of us were laboring with heavy metal folding chairs and tables, we all turned right toward the gym. Kip, the last to leave the room, with his winter coat now on and fully zipped up, turned left, with both hands placed in a supporting mode at belt level, facing upward under his coat. Clearly he had the Pickett's hidden in his coat, but I couldn't fathom why on Earth he was heading to church with it. Did he not know God could see everything that entered the church, coat covered or not? I was convinced the boy had lost it!

Kip disappeared down the tunnel, up the stairs to the church, and out of our sight. About fifteen minutes later, he joined the rest of us as we lined up outside of the doors to school, awaiting the morning bell that would send us marching inside in pairs. We all knew Kip had nabbed the beer, but we had no idea what he had done with it. At recess that morning, as we all headed out for fifteen minutes of snowball fights and group conversations on the blacktop parking lot of the school, those of us who had been on table and chair duty that morning huddled around Kip like bees on honey.

"Where's the Pickett's?" asked Jungo.

"I'm not sure," replied Kip, lying through his teeth. "I headed into the church and was going to hide it under the altar, but Father O'Brien saw me and asked me where I was going with it. I told him I was taking it to the storage room at the direction of Sister Paschal, but he said he would handle that, so I gave it up, and he walked back to the rectory with it."

At the news the beer had been confiscated, the group let out a collective moan.

"Oh no!" yelled Jungo.

"You have got to be kidding," replied Kinger.

"What beer?" questioned Tom Crimmins, who had just wandered up to the huddle and whose dad, Ralph, managed the bingo supplies for the church council. Just then, the bell for class rang, and we all darted back into school, ignoring Crimmins's question and avoiding any response.

Kip sat next to me in Mr. Osterberger's U.S. history class after recess. A few minutes after we pulled out our books, Kip leaned over to whisper something to me. "Nooch," he said across the aisle, calling me by the nickname I was given at school, but different from the one the neighborhood guys called me, "I have the Pickett's."

I was not the least bit surprised. I knew Kip better than anyone else at school, and I knew he was lying when he told the group on the playground the false outcome of the allegedly missing brew.

Just then, a loud and stern voice bellowed through the room. It was that of the male lay teacher patriarch of the school, Jim Osterberger (whom we called 'Ostey' behind his back), and he was not to be messed with. "Mr. Kane, Mr. Neuhaus, is there something you two would like to share with the class?"

"No, sir," I said. "Kip was just asking if I would come over to his house tonight to study, that's all." It was only a half-lie, as I had every intention of going to Kip's house that night, though studying had nothing to do with it.

After school, I caught up with Kipper on the football practice field, dying to know what had become of the Pickett's Premium. Kip informed me he had tucked it in a small open box area under the altar inside the church. We had to retrieve the contraband before Mass at six a.m. the next morning, because the attending priest would surely notice the twelve-pack near his feet on the side of the altar that only faced him, opposite the congregation.

The church was a great hideout spot for us kids, particularly in the winter, when the doors were unlocked until about midnight. It was quiet, warm, and usually uninhabited. We frequently went inside to escape the evening winter chill when we were out wandering around the neighborhood. We also found the vacant, dark confessional to be an outstanding place to slip into with one of the girls from school for a brief make-out session.

Kip knew he could not bring the beer out into daylight the morning of the heist, so he tucked it under the church altar. Unlike the school that was locked most nights by five p.m., he knew the church would be open and empty well into the evening. That evening, after meeting up at Kip's house after dinner (and not studying), we wandered into church, walked up the center aisle, genuflected before the statue of Jesus, and sat quietly, pretending to be in silent prayer while we scoped out the House of the Lord to make sure there were no onlookers. After a few minutes, we decided the coast was clear, and Kip jogged from the pew up to the altar. He reached underneath and pulled out the 'twelver'. We bolted from Nativity Church into the cold, dark night, with visions of drunkenness dancing in our heads.

We couldn't risk taking the beer into either of our homes, so we decided to stash it under some bushes in a yard across the street from the church. We swore in blood brother-like fashion that neither of us would mention this to a soul, at least until we figured out when and where we would pop the first top and who we would include in the adventure. We checked on the beer each night during the week to make sure it had not been discovered. During our last check of the week, on Thursday night, all was still cool. The beer was there, and the next day was Friday—the perfect time to start an underage bender.

CHAPTER 36

Fiasco at the Field House

When school let out on Friday, Kip and I grabbed Jungo and Kinger and told them to come with us over to Kip's house to hang out. When we got to Kip's, we revealed to our expanded brethren the resurrection of the brew that had been long forgotten after Kip's recess lie about Father O'Brien intercepting that Monday. We were all giddy with anticipation and delight, as we schemed about where we would consume our forbidden treasure.

Just a short block from Nativity School and Church was the Loras College campus. A favorite activity for us during the winter was to attend the Loras College Duhawk basketball games in the old Fieldhouse, the college gym. We decided the best plan would be to wait until dark, then wander to the yard where the beer was stashed in the bushes, take it down under the dormant concession stand at the Rock Bowl (the college football field), and get our fill before entering the basketball game. And that is what we did.

When we arrived at the Rock Bowl around six thirty p.m. that February evening, it may as well have been the middle of a cornfield. There was a foot of heavy white snow covering the playing field and the bleachers. The concession stand had been locked up after the last football game in November and had remained dormant ever since. A winter wind blew through the fifty-foot blue spruce trees that lined the far sideline of the field, and not a soul would be anywhere near there until the spring thaw came the next month and the track team would reclaim the track that encircled the field for their practices. We had found the perfect private place to unleash the pent-up demand from a week of waiting.

Pishhhht! Pishhhht! Pishhhht! Pishhhht! went the four popped cans and to our lips went the cold aluminum cans wrapped in each of our right-hand gloves. Down went the first beers in a chugging contest, followed abruptly by a series of burps. Kipper won. The next beers went down considerably slower and with far less enthusiasm.

When we finished our beers, three each, it was time to head up the stairs of the abandoned stadium, around the corner, and down the walk toward the Fieldhouse. By now, it was nearly seven thirty p.m. and time for tipoff. A steady flow of pedestrian traffic had begun to make its way in the heavy wooden doors of the old brick building, whose illumination from prehistoric metal and fluorescent lights poured out the hand-cranked paneled windows that were left open even in the winter to keep the outdated landmark from overheating the crowd of 1,000 or so that would assemble for the evening contest.

As we stumbled in the doors and paid our one-dollar admission, bumping into one another and bouncing clumsily off of people nearby us in line who seemed a bit annoyed by our antics, we could not control our giggling and joking. We had indulged and were feeling the effects. We wondered how people could do this on Monday night and still keep track of a set of bingo cards. We came to the conclusion that bingo players were excellent at multitasking.

The Loras Fieldhouse had two oval-shaped levels, both with stacked bleacher seating. Floor level surrounded the court, and the front row of spectators were so close to the action that they had to pull their feet out of the way when play came down the sidelines. The upper level had a green metal railing that mimicked the oval shape of the building, separating the first row of the upstairs bleachers from the open drop of about twenty feet down to the court and the team benches. We always sat in the first row upstairs, immediately overlooking the opponents' bench. It was the prime position in the house for heckling the visiting players and coaches, and that was something we immensely enjoyed even on our more sober days.

This particular night, the Duhawks were playing Parsons College. Parsons was the joke of the league, and the school actually ended up closing down in the mid-1970's as a result of lackluster enrollment. We contended it was because of their gaudy basketball uniforms, which were something of a cross between the Harlem Globetrotters and a clown costume. The poor ballers from Parsons were forced to wear crazy stripes and colors that were just all-around ugly.

Throughout the first half of the game, we yelled rude names at the Parsons players and coaches and screamed and whistled when they were shooting free throws. Even with the home Duhawks up by about twenty-five points at the half, we were relentless in our verbal assault. One of the memories I will always associate with the old Loras Fieldhouse was the tantalizing aroma of hot buttery popcorn that was popped fresh throughout the game in an old-fashioned giant popper, the kind with a big metal red base that rose about halfway up, with see-through glass windows and two doors on the front that would swing open, letting out the bright yellow rays from the heat lamp that kept the delicious stuff fresh and tasty. Walking in the front doors of the field house for a basketball game was the aromatic equivalent of walking into a movie theater, and it was impossible to forego the butter-soaked yellow corn. At halftime of every game, it was popcorn for all.

While the wounded Parsons squad dragged their already defeated rear ends to the locker room for inspiration and to develop a plan for attempting to overcome the deep deficit in which they were mired, Kipper, Yungo, Kinger, and I all headed for the popcorn stand, returning moments later to our perch above the visitors' bench just in time to see the teams return to the court for warm-ups prior to the start of the second half. As we munched on our snacks from our overflowing, grease-stained white paper bags, I noticed that Kipper had fallen a bit silent and had stopped eating his popcorn. Just then, the buzzer from the scorer's table sounded abruptly, indicating the start of the second half.

As the Parsons starting five strutted out to center court in their ridiculous clown garb and the reserves strolled leisurely toward their bench directly below our dangling boots, I turned to Kip and asked if he was okay. Kip turned his head toward me to attempt a response and opened his mouth to speak, but no words came out. Before I could ask what was wrong, I realized his face was white as a ghost. I knew immediately what was to follow, but I was unable to respond with any preventative action. Kip stood abruptly, bent over the rail, and spewed about a quart of recycled beer and two handfuls of half-digested popcorn forcefully and directly down on the Parsons' bench. The players who were within a few steps of the bench looked up and jumped back as Kip's offering to them hit the empty bench, splattering about ten feet out onto the floor and decorating several of the players warm-up bottoms and shoes with an unexpected soaking. I grabbed Kip by the arm, and we all got up and ran for the backdoor stairs, exiting the Fieldhouse and running out into the moonlit winter night to avoid the wrath of the old potbellied, gray-haired Loras security guard who knew us well and was certain to pursue us across the Keane Hall field in his four-wheel drive Jeep. Pursue he did, but we ducked into the nearby planetarium, where a show about the stars and planets of the winter sky was being narrated by one of the Loras science professors. The Jeep sped by, never to apprehend the puking prankster. Later, we learned Kip had neglected to eat that day, so three chugged beers and a little greasy popcorn did not sit well with his insides. We made mental notes for future reference, enjoyed the planetarium show, and headed home to our warm and cozy beds, eager to enjoy sleeping in since the next morning was a Saturday.

CHAPTER 37

College Kids

From about the fifth through eighth grades, my Nativity gang friends and I treated the Loras College campus as our own extended playground. We stole a peek at our futures while observing and interacting with eighteen to twenty-one year-olds. They behaved a lot differently than those of us who were twelve or thirteen, and we found the Loras students' lifestyles to be intriguing and alluring. They seemed to come and go as they pleased, with no parents to rule their lives. They had their own dorm rooms, and many of them had their own cars. They wandered many nights and weekends down Loras Boulevard to Phil's Pizza Place and up to University Avenue to the bars such as The Avenue Tap ('The Ave'), The Walnut Tap ('The Nut'), and The Cardinal Tap (which had no nickname that I ever knew about). They went to campus sporting events, had all kinds of campus festivals, dance marathons, and played pick-up flag football and softball games on the many green campus recreation areas. We were excited about our upcoming college years, though it seemed like it was a lifetime away. We settled for the next best thing; we lived it vicariously by hanging out on the campus.

Some of the Loras students were friendly toward us and sort of treated us as adopted kid brothers and sisters, perhaps as surrogate replacements for the younger siblings they had left behind in the rural Iowa towns and Chicago suburbs where they had spent most of their lives growing up before heading off to college. We looked up to some of these big buddies and loved to pretend we were older than we were when we were around them. Other Loras students seemed to resent the presence of kids on campus and made no bones about letting us know we were not welcome. For that bunch, we had special ways of reciprocating our mutual disinterest.

Back in the days before dorm rooms all had mini-fridges, it was not uncommon for the college students to set their six-packs of Schlitz, Falstaff, or Hamm's out on the cement ledge at the base of the window to their rooms to keep them cool. Perhaps it was sheer coincidence that those who refused to be hospitable to us would experience severe beer losses in the dark of the night. For the ones we really detested, not only would we steal their beer off the ledge, but we would also wait for them to open their window, notice the beer was gone and instinctively tilt their heads down, thinking the cans had fallen of the ledge, and at that very moment, we would fire about a dozen snowballs at them and into their dorm room. We ran like hell as they screamed obscenities at us and pulled on their boots to scramble down a few flights of stairs, thinking they could catch us. Our predators never did catch us. After all, this was our neighborhood, our turf, and they were merely visitors passing through. We grew up there. We knew every alley, every backyard, and every unlocked garage or building to hide in. College kids or not, they had no chance of catching up to a bunch of junior high pranksters.

I recall once walking down a long flight of stairs in one of the buildings at Loras. The stairwell had been filled in with white cement block as a safety precaution to keep people from falling over the rail from four or five flights above. On the bright white block, a student had scribbled some graffiti in dark black magic marker: 'If you can't dazzle 'em with brilliance, baffle 'em with bullshit'. We pondered that saying for a while, and the more we thought about it, the more we realized it was pretty much how we survived the daily regimen of discipline and structure at Nativity School and Church. We talked our way out of a lot of awkward situations with the teachers, nuns, priests, our parents, and even the old gray-haired security guard who drove his Jeep around the Loras campus as a result of the exposure we had to the older college kids we mimicked. Yeah, those college kids were learning something over there at Loras, and we were benefitting from the morsels of wisdom we would occasionally pick up and carry with us. We were certainly learning to baffle 'em with bullshit.

Of all the Loras students we encountered during our many escapades about the campus, the one who most impacted my life, by far, was a young man by the name of Walter Truby. The Loras students we met almost all lived on campus, but Walt rented the basement studio apartment in the triplex building right across the back alley from 116. When he moved out of the dorms, he became, for all intents and purposes, our new neighbor.

Walt Truby was a mature, bright, good-looking, and career-focused young man. I suspect after a year in the dorms, he was ready to move beyond the child's play that could carry on for many students well into their junior or senior years. This was not for Walt. The college sophomore from Grayslake, Illinois, a suburb of Chicago, drove a brand new royal blue Ford Mustang. My brother Tom might have had the Hot Wheels version, but Walt had the real thing, and it was an oh-so-sweet car. We used to come out with our hose and sponges when we saw Walt getting ready to wash the beauty because we knew our likely reward was going to be a ride to the A&W Drive-in on Dodge Street for a root beer when we were done. I don't know what was better, the ride in the coolest car on Earth or the A&W experience. From Turtle Wax to an icy, frothy mug, the whole deal was just an absolute treat.

Much like Dave Brown, another college student who years later ended up being one of my football coaches when I entered the eighth grade at Nativity, Walt Truby was one of those people who always had something good to say about everyone, right to their face, to make them feel special. He was also on to Ken's bullying and didn't mind expressing his disapproval of it to my older brother from time to time. Walt volunteered to umpire our neighborhood baseball games, took us to Dubuque Packer games, played games with us in the front yard of his apartment and of 116, and was always just a really great guy to be around.

We were all heartbroken when the landlord found a note on Walt's apartment one day asking him to let us all know he had been drafted and was to be shipped off to Vietnam. He apologized in the letter for not saying goodbye in person, but explained it would have just been too difficult, and he hoped we would understand. Walt had become a part of our family in many ways, and just like that, he was gone. He was my hero . . . and in Vietnam, I'm sure he became a hero to a lot of other young men as well.

CHAPTER 38

Ken Comes Around

Although the college students we shadowed on the Loras campus certainly exposed us to life beyond our years, they were not the only role models we had that aided in our education of things to come. There were older siblings, like Kathy and Laura King, who were quite adept at that, and we savored the opportunity to study the lessons of life under their tutelage.

While my brother Ken was a challenging figure to deal with in the earliest of years at 116, he evolved over time, as people do when they mature, into a different person, and it allowed our relationship to take on new dimensions. The year after Ken graduated from high school and I was in the eighth grade, he moved out into his own apartment. Things between Ken and me began to look up. He underwent a transformation, in my eyes, from tyrant to totally cool buddy and big brother. When he came over to 116 for visits, free meals, or laundry assistance, we enjoyed one another's company, and he seemed genuinely interested in what was going on in my life. I began to look up to him just as we did the Loras students, and I even started to envy him and his newfound freedom.

One winter evening, on a Friday night, Ken was having a party at his apartment and he invited Kipper, Kinger, and me to attend. We were all sworn to secrecy, of course, as there would be a keg of beer at the party, and it was important that no one outside the party know he allowed us access to the devil's brew. We understood the rules and were flattered to be trusted amongst an older group of people. Ken told us to come over anytime after eight p.m. We could not have been more excited about it.

We met up at Kip's house after dinner that evening and waited as the clock slowly, ever so slowly, moved from six p.m. to seven-thirty, when we agreed it was time to set out on the thirty minute walk across several neighborhoods to Ken's pad. We ventured from Kip's place, up Alpine Street, and across the Nativity School parking lot. From there, we crossed behind the church to Booth Street and followed that, crossing Loras Boulevard, and then hiking into some woods that bordered Glen Oak Street. It was a frigid and dark winter evening, and the frozen, icy path through the woods crackled with each step we took. There was no moonlight to illuminate our trek, so visibility in the woods was minimal, giving off a spooky ambiance. We were not too bothered, however, because we were together, focused on the destination that awaited us. We knew there would be beer, rock 'n' roll, eight-track tapes, and girls four and five years older than us. We were on a mission for fun, and no obstacle would stand in our way—that is, until we emerged from the woods onto Grandview Avenue, where we encountered Bruce Biederman and his gang of outcasts. We were within about four blocks of Ken's apartment, but doubt was suddenly cast upon us.

Bruce Biederman was an oversized, twenty-something bully. Unlike Ken, Bruce had not matured to the next stage of life. He stood about six-two and weighed in excess of 300 pounds. He always wore a Daniel Boone sort of fur hat, an army green parka jacket, and steel-toed black boots that should have been registered as lethal weapons. At his side stood three of his yes-men. "What are you little shits doing cutting through our woods?" Bruce challenged.

"Yeah! What do you think you're doin' around here?" and similar such echoes murmured from the pack as they began to move within a few feet of us.

Without responding to the meritless verbiage that was only intended to entrap us, we all retreated in panicked fashion, back into the woods, with the older troublemakers in full pursuit. We held two advantages over our opponents, and we knew we had to exercise both immediately. We were faster, and we knew our ultimate destination. As we scurried back into the woods, our hearts pounding as we pushed tree branches away from our faces with every stride, I shouted to my companions, "Meet at Ken's!" At that, we scattered three different directions, hopeful that none of us would be chased down and ganged up on in a four-on-one brawl.

When I got to Ken's place, I stopped at the foot of the long, narrow wooden staircase that led up to the second-floor apartment. I was huffing and puffing, bent over at the waist with my hands on my knees, my lungs burning from the cold air that had assaulted them during the escape from the pack of madmen (or mad boys, as it were). As I began to compose myself, my thoughts turned to the wellbeing of my partners in supposed trespassing crime. I wondered if Kipper and Kinger had made a clean escape. As I pondered their possible fates, I noticed movement in the evergreen bushes across the street, an animal perhaps? Then, out from the snow-covered bushes, popped a navy blue stocking cap. The head beneath it looked both ways up and down the sidewalk. It was Kipper, Kinger in tow stumbling out of the camouflage behind him. We were reunited and ready to continue our quest for the good life. All systems were go, and we headed up the stairs to Ken's apartment in search of a party.

As we pulled open the aluminum storm door and entered Ken's place, the KISS tune, "I Wanna Rock and Roll All Night" blasted across the room. *How appropriate,* I thought, sure the party was gonna be an unforgettable experience from start to finish and glad we had made it there alive.

Ken's place was packed shoulder to shoulder with a mix of underage drinkers who had just departed a dance at the nearby high school, as well as a number of eighteen—and nineteen-year-olds who were barely removed from that scene but had reached the magical drinking age in Iowa at that time. It seemed only fitting that anyone who was old enough to vote or go to war was old enough to tie a few on now and again.

Virtually everyone in the apartment was drinking from clear plastic cups filled with golden liquid, foam floating on the top. One guy, Kenny Rapp, who apparently had appointed himself the official provider of beer for all, staggered through the crowd with two glass pitchers, one in each hand, stopping at every cup that was less than half full and topping them off. We later surmised that 'Ripper', as he was called, was on some kind of quest for acceptance and popularity with the girls at the party. Whatever goodwill or favor he had won with the girls for his roving antics were all for naught, as he passed out before ten and instead of wandering off with one of his lovely customers to a bedroom, took single occupancy of one of the rooms for the rest of the night, much to the dismay of a number of the other people on the prowl for love that night. Before making his untimely exit for the evening, Ripper did manage to provide my eighth-grade buddies and me with the cups we required for participation in the fest. "Viva la Ripper!" we toasted. "May he rest in peace."

The rock music was loud, and the conversations were broken and generally incoherent in the apartment that night. Our attempts to attract older women proved difficult, as we had to shout our clever come-ons over the blaring lyrics of the Doobie Brothers' "Black Water" and Bachman Turner Overdrive's "Takin' Care of Business." Our efforts were less than fruitful. While many of the girls talked and flirted with us, we found it was more out of a sense of novelty or amusement that there were miniature partiers in the house. We later reflected on what the interactions were about and concluded they were less about an interest in us personally and more comparable to putting beer in your dog's water bowl to see how a tipsy pooch would act. It was just an experiment, of sorts, and we were the drunken puppies, there to entertain everyone.

While Kipper sat on the couch trying to impress a high school senior girl by telling her how many points he had scored for the Nativity Royals in a basketball game vs. Holy Ghost earlier that week and Kinger was at the kitchen table being suckered by some of the older guys at the party into a game of quarters, a heart-stopping scene began to play out at the door to the apartment. The men in blue had arrived! Kinger was about to chug his third straight beer, much to the laughter and delight of the older partiers, who, as it turned out, were quite proficient in the art of bouncing quarters into cups of beer, when I grabbed him by the collar and pulled him out of his chair, exclaiming at the top of my lungs, "The cops are here!" The party was under siege. There was going to be a bust, and suddenly, Ken's apartment was no place for three fourteen-year-olds. We needed to get out, and fast.

As the two police officers wandered the crowd in search of the proprietor, my brother Ken turned off the stereo, and the formerly rockin' funfest that was his living room fell utterly silent.

Every town in America has that one member of the local police department, who, for whatever twisted reason, seems to take extreme satisfaction in busting young people. In Dubuque, that guy was Leo Lynch. Maybe he never got invited to parties when he was young and this was his version of Revenge of the Nerds. Whatever the case, it did not bode well for the underage group at the party that night that not only the police had arrived, but Leo Lynch, the 'Kid Buster', was in the house.

Leo and his partner instructed everyone to sit down while they systematically moved through the crowd, notebooks and pens in hand, checking IDs and recording names and addresses of anyone who was not of legal age. Each time the authorities moved closer to where Kip, Kinger, and I stood in the corner of the kitchen near the stove, we would take a few more steps in the other direction, allowing other, older people to be shaken down ahead of us. As we felt the inevitable gap closing upon us, we opted to make a slow and casual move toward the door. We hoped the cops would keep too busy with their notepads and pens to notice our subtle movement, but it was not to be. "Hold up there, little men," we heard Leo command, and it was then that we knew our number was up.

The fifty-something, stern, dark-haired and intimidating police figure stared us down with piercing eyes. None of the three of us had ever experienced such a degree of horror, not even under the glare of our fathers. We had learned from the Loras students how to baffle them with you know what, and it worked well with the priests, nuns, and teachers at Nativity—even with our parents some of the time—but we knew instinctively that the price of poker had gone up, and bluffing was not an option. We were clearly out of our league with Leo Lynch, and straightforward confession was the only way to go. But we had momentarily forgotten that Kipper was amongst us.

Leo started the questioning with Kip. He asked his name, age, and address.

Kipper led off with the wit and cunning attitude for which he was so well known among the Nativity gang. Kip replied, "I'm Joe Fleckenstein, fourteen years old, and I live at 1380 St. Ambrose Street." Joe was, in fact, one of our rivals from St. Anthony's, the neighborhood we were in at the party apartment.

Kinger followed Kip's lead. "I'm Dan Donovan, fourteen, 2345 Hillcrest Road."

I finished the interrogation, claiming to be John McCarthy, another fourteen-year-old St. Anthony's rival who also lived in the neighborhood.

Kip's opening was brilliant on a couple of counts. First, when Officer Unfriendly asked us what we were doing at this party with older people, we were able to say we didn't know anyone there and simply heard the loud music and wandered in uninvited. It was believable since we appeared to be close to our homes. Second, it allowed me to protect my brother Ken by avoiding the disclosure of any relationship between us or his guilt in inviting minors to the party. And third, it gave us the best chance at being allowed to leave on our own free will, since we all could allegedly walk just a few blocks to our homes.

After serving dutifully and respectfully as the targets of an arsenal of the predictable, but nonetheless, painful harassment techniques upon which Lynch had built his reputation, he directed us to go straight home and told us we would find out what the food tasted like in the Dubuque jail if we deviated, even slightly, from his very clear and rigid directive. We told him we would do just that and thanked him for his kind act of leniency, insisting we had learned a valuable lesson.

Once again, Kip pulled off only what Kip could, and we were free men . . . or free boys, as it were.

Our adrenaline rush shot us down the stairs and across Grandview Avenue, where we looked both ways for Bruce Biederman and his mad pack before proceeding back into the woods toward what several times during the course of the adventurous evening appeared to be an unlikely safe and triumphant return to our home Nativity turf. The beer was okay, the girls were great, and the escape was miraculous, but the best part was that it came with the unknowing help of our St. Anthony's rivals. All in all, it was sweet!

Kipper, Kinger, and I still had a pretty good beer buzz on by the time we reached the Nativity School parking lot around ten-thirty that evening. It's not that our intoxicated state had ever gone away, just that the focus on the need to perform under intense scrutiny had crushed it a bit, to where it was subconscious for a while. We were feeling it again and were quite giddy about the way we had fooled Leo Lynch. Kinger's girlfriend was Annie McKay, Kipper had the hots for Lisa Kingsley, and Julie Hoffmann and I had pretty much been a couple on and off for the better part of sixth, seventh, and eighth grades. We knew the girls had all gone to Mary Kuehnle's house for one of the boy/girl dance parties Mary's parents often allowed her to host in the furnished basement/recreation room of their home. Since we had struck out in grand fashion in our attempt to play among the girls of the big leagues at Ken's place, we were suddenly accepting and grateful to return to the minor leagues. Julie, Annie, and Lisa would know nothing of our failed efforts and would be pleased we had shown up in time for a few slow dances with the basement lights dimmed before eleven rolled around and

Mr. Kuehnle would come downstairs to let us know it was time to bid our farewells for the night.

We jogged through the school parking lot, down a couple sets of cement stairs to the Booth Street entrance to the campus, and across Booth Street to Mary Kuehnle's house. It was as close to school as anyone could want to live, and that made it a popular hangout for most of the eighth grade.

We slipped in the basement side door of Kuehnle's unexpectedly, only to find our girls dancing with Pie Man Crimmins, Beanie Botsford, and Shleets—a seventh grader, mind you! If we had been wearing shoes, one might say they had been placed on the proverbial other foot, but we had taken our snow and slush covered boots off at the door like the mature gentlemen we thought ourselves to be. Still, we were indeed experiencing the feeling of the shoe being on the other foot. Dance cards changed in quick order as we reclaimed our partners. We told everyone the story of our evening, and they were quite impressed. When Mr. Kuehnle flashed the basement lights on and off twice, the signal that the dance party was over, Julie asked if I would walk her home. I was more than thrilled to do so, as I knew very well that my reward would be one of Julie's slow and wet kisses under the apple tree behind the Mt. Pleasant old folks' home, which sat just above Wood Street and across the street from her parents' residence. We left Mary's hand in hand—or mitten in glove, as Iowa winters would have it. I was glad to have her at my side and away from Shleets's.

CHAPTER 39

Viva la France

Mary Kuehnle's basement was but one of a number of venues whereby the Nativity boys sought to hook up with the Nativity girls. Other popular spots to sneak in a kiss, hold hands, or snuggle up included: Skate Country, the local roller-skating rink; Alison Henderson Park outdoor ice-skating rink; the Loras College planetarium; the confessional at Nativity Church; and my favorite, under the apple tree in the secluded back field/garden of the Mt. Pleasant old folk's home. The one thing all of these locations had in common is that they were dimly lit or afforded a degree of privacy that was hard to find just anywhere.

A sure way for a Royal girl to know if a Royal boy had a thing for her was for the girl to sit on the bench in the warming house at Alison Henderson when others were out ice-skating. This is where the question, "Do you want to go around the rink with me?" was often popped. If a guy and girl held hands while going around the ice-skating circle, it was a signal to all other callers that they had to look elsewhere. Though a few St. Anthony's kids showed up now and then, it was pretty much dominated by Nativity kids.

Skate Country was one of those West End developments that popped up a short while after Kennedy Mall. It was the first and only indoor roller-skating rink, and it was hugely popular with the eleven to fourteen year old crowds from all the schools in town. This was where a lot of intra-school flirting among the genders went down. Skate Country was great because it was dark, except for the colored disco ball and strobe lights that flashed to the sound of slowed-down rock music as we skated around the oval-shaped tile track with whatever girl we could get the nerve up to ask. More than a few catfights erupted among the girls from the different schools when someone felt someone else was moving in on their guy, and there was always some apprehension as to what retaliatory response might be evoked from a St. Columbkille's guy or a St. Anthony's guy if a Nativity guy were seen hand in hand with a girl from one of their schools. The sure sign of a serious courtship between two young skaters from any school was indicated by whom they skated with when the Moody Blues song "Nights in White Satin" was played. It was slow, long, romantic, and dropped, in lyrical form, the phrase "I love you" about fifty times. Yeah, that was the tell-all song.

The Loras planetarium was another fine hookup spot. It was a silo-shaped, one-level building that had movie theatre-type chairs arranged in circular fashion, about eight rows deep. The ceiling of the building served as a screen for the projector, which emitted a simulation of the night sky, including the stars, constellations, and planets that could be identified in the real night sky at that particular time of the year. The lights were off for the entire show, and everyone was leaning back in their chairs, heads looking up at the ceiling the entire hour or so while the narrator described what to look for in the sky with his little white pointer light. While everyone was looking up in the dark, it was the perfect time to make out for pretty much as long as you wanted, or at least until the house lights came back up for the question-and-answer part of the program. By that time, though, our gang was always long gone.

The confessional at Nativity Church was a great spot for exploring the desires that came with the onset of puberty. The doors to the church were open at least until midnight and sometimes all night. A couple of us would sit or kneel in one of the pews, standing watch, while the couple whose turn it was to enter the pitch-dark booth for a frolic of their choosing would take their five minutes or so of action time. We rotated shifts, and it worked well for everyone. The stories the boys told the other boys about what they had done with their partner in the confessional were always quite embellished, but it made for good gossip. Of course, it was never good to find out the next day that the exaggerated tales had made it back to the person who had been in the booth with you.

Last but not least, the apple tree behind the Mt. Pleasant old folk's home was my favorite. Truth be known, there was only one girl I ever kissed under that tree. It was where I received my first kiss and the most kisses during the Nativity days, and it was always with Julie Hoffmann. Julie was an advanced kisser. We were pretty sure she was spending some side time with high school boys even when we were just in the eighth grade, but we didn't talk about it. One night I will never forget, we were kissing goodnight and Julie asked, "Do you want to French?"

I had not the slightest idea what she was talking about. I thought she was asking me if I had been to France or something like that, and I must have looked at her with a strange expression on my face because she just stared at me and the night fell silent. For a moment, our connection was lost.

Being patient with me, she worded it another way. "Kiss. You know, French kiss."

"Oh," I said. "Sure, I can do that," though I still didn't have the foggiest idea what she was talking about.

As our lips met again, I felt the slip of her wet tongue into my mouth and could taste in great detail, the flavor of her Leaf brand sour grape bubble gum, that at this point, I was all but chewing myself! Things had just gone to the next level. Julie Hoffmann had put her tongue in my mouth and rolled it around, side to side and up and down. Julie was so proficient in this technique that I questioned whether or not I would really need to brush my teeth before bed that night. On the long walk home that evening, I was absolutely jacked with excitement, replaying in my mind what had gone on and unable to contain myself with the thought of telling the guys at school the next day about my latest tryst with Julie. It was quite an ordeal and begged the breach of the kiss-and-tell rule.

Suddenly, a scary thought occurred to me. What if I can get VD from Frenching! I didn't really know what it was, but based on the context in which I had heard it mentioned here and there, I knew it was not something I wanted. "Please, God, don't let me get VD from French kissing Julie Hoffmann" was my bedtime prayer that night. There was no way I was going to even whisper this one to the priest at confession, and I certainly wasn't going to ask Aunt Agnes to join me in that prayer.

CHAPTER 40

Sex Education

In order to understand why, at the age of almost fourteen, I wondered if I might catch a venereal disease from French kissing Julie Hoffmann, it might be good to do a root cause analysis of the problem. The concept of conducting a root cause analysis, of course, theorizes that actions that result in problems at a particular point in time have roots, or beginnings, that start considerably earlier in time than at the point where the problem manifests. Indeed, that was the case with my understanding of VD.

For years in the late 1960's and early 1970's, there was a good deal of debate among Catholic leaders and educators as to how much, if any, sex education should be delivered in school settings and what age was appropriate for introducing the birds and the bees.

At Nativity School, a decision was made (I suppose by the church and school governing board) to begin to inform students about the details of sex in the seventh grade. I recall one day, Jim Osterberger, Ostey, sequestered all the boys in the class to the school library. Mrs. Fitzpatrick, meanwhile, took all the girls to the staging area in the lower gymnasium. None of us really knew what was going on, but it was obvious something was going to happen for the first time, because the separation of the genders at school was highly unusual.

When the thirty-five or so boys were settled in the library, which had now been closed to the rest of the school, Ostey began the introduction of the unit by explaining some basic differences between the genders. It was then that we knew where this was going, and it was not a place most of us wanted to go—at least not sitting in a school library. After this first one-hour introductory session, Ostey explained that there was a record in the library we each had to check out and listen to one night with our parents sometime during the following six weeks and then return it with a form that our parents were to sign, indicating that we had completed the listening assignment together. Only after completing the parent accompanied listening exercise, and with evidence of their express consent, would we be allowed to continue on with the sessions at school.

We were relieved when the session was over, but filled with anxiety about the weeks to come. The most frightening thing for the moment, however, was getting up the nerve to walk into the library sometime over the next few weeks and ask Mrs. Kingsley, the librarian and also the mother of Lisa, a girl in our class who all the boys were interested in, to check the record out to us. Will she think we were dirty? Will she warn us not to try anything we hear on the record with her daughter? Will she laugh at us? All of this and more cluttered our minds.

After a week or so, and having chatted with a few guys who had completed the task, I got the nerve up to ask Mrs. Kingsley for the record. I practiced a number of times how I would ask her and thought about how I would answer any potential questions she might ask me. It was now time for action. I walked into the library, prepared to ask the question, but as I approached her desk, a couple of the girls in my class appeared in line behind me and were waiting to check out books. Oh Lord, I thought. I can't have them overhearing this.

Mrs. Kingsley looked at me and asked, "Roger, do you have a book to check out?"

I told her I had left it on the reading table and would be right back, but she should go ahead and serve the girls first, and I would wait. I waited until the girls were gone before I headed back to Mrs. Kingsley's desk with a book in my hand that I had randomly grabbed off a shelf without even looking. I set the book before Mrs. Kingsley and told her I would like to check it out. For a moment, I considered abandoning the record request and postponing it to another day.

Mrs. Kingsley looked at the book I had selected and then looked over the top of her glasses questioningly at me. "Dr. Seuss' *The Cat in the Hat?*" she inquired.

My thoughts preoccupied, I had inadvertently grabbed the book from the second-grade bookshelf. "Oh yeah," I said. "I'm going to take it home and read it to my little sister," I lied. "And by the way," I slipped in ever so quickly and quietly, "I also need to check out the record . . . you know, for the boys only?"

Mrs. Kingsley was ever so understanding of my situation as she placed the now checked-out Seuss book back in my hands. "Both copies of the record are checked out right now, Roger, but I'll put you next on the waiting list and notify you when one comes back. I hope your sister likes the book. You're a good brother," she finished.

"That's fine," I replied, like it was no big deal. Then I headed for the library exit with a great sense of urgency to just get out of there as soon possible.

When I reached the hallway and started walking by the lockers on my way back to class, I lamented all the effort I had put into the fruitless attempt at securing the sex record and felt a complete sense of failure for not being any closer to having the bothersome task behind me.

All the classrooms at Nativity School had, placed above the blackboard, in the front and center of the room, an enclosed, wooden-framed speaker box with black nylon-like fabric stretched over the front of it. The box distributed sound to the rooms in the form of announcements that were broadcast from a microphone in the principal's office.

As I sat at my desk listening to the morning announcements a few days after my encounter with Mrs. Kingsley, I heard the school lunch menu for the day announced, a rundown of which boys' and girls' teams had after-school games that day and then, the librarian. I didn't think anything of it at first because it was common for Mrs. Kingsley to announce a list of people who had overdue books and the fines that would be assessed if the books were not returned immediately. But this day, much to my chagrin, there would be a customized message. At the end of the announcements, Mrs. Kingsley added, almost as an afterthought, "Oh . . . if Roger Neuhaus is listening, the record you have been waiting to check out is now available. I'll hold it for you."

Everyone in my class, boys and girls alike, knew which record it was. I slumped in my seat and began to feel my face heat up as blood rushed to my head, wanting nothing more than to get on with class.

Later that day, I went and checked out the much-dreaded record. It was amazingly simple this time since the whole school already knew I was doing it, and there was no one I needed to try and hide it from.

Walking home from school that day, my apprehension about the record turned from school focused to home focused. I had no idea how to bring this up to my parents. Should I tell my mom? My dad? Them both? How should I present this? "Um, say Ken and Mary, your sex fiend seventh grader wants to listen to a sex record, and you're supposed to join me in the fun." Maybe not, but that's what it felt like I was going to have to say. Oh God! Maybe I could just forge my parents' signatures and take the record back unplayed. No. I need to get the courage up to do this.

After dinner, when my mom was in the kitchen doing the dishes and the rest of the family was doing homework or watching TV, I seized a private moment to approach my mother and just blurted it out. "Hey, Mom, I have this dumb record all the boys at school have to listen to with their parents. Can you, me, and Dad do this real quick?"

"That won't be necessary," Mary replied. "We heard it two years ago when your brother Tom was in seventh grade, so you can just take it back tomorrow."

I stood befuddled as my mother gazed directly at the dishwater, unable to even make eye contact with me. I wanted to tell her I needed to hear it, but that would have made me sound like some kind of pervert, or at least I thought so. After a few silent moments, I told my mom she had to sign a form saying we had listened to the record together. I presented her the form, and she signed both names to it, changing the subject by asking if I had some homework to do. My unspoken mental answer was "I did, but not anymore."

A week or two later, after everyone had supposedly listened to the record, Ostey told us we would be continuing with our group sessions the next day. That night at home, I became ill with the stomach flu and was as sick as a dog, vomiting and unable to keep anything down. I stayed home from school in the morning, but told Mom I was feeling better and could join my classmates after lunch for the second half of the school day. The truth was that I really did not feel that much better, but we had a basketball game against Holy Ghost that day after school, and we were only allowed to play if we had been in school at least half the day. I needed to play in that game, so I persevered and made it to school by twelve-thirty p.m.

At one-thirty, Ostey chaperoned the boys to the library for another session of sex education. Many of the guys actually had questions about what they had heard on the record and were brave enough to ask them, but not me. Nevertheless, to cover up my failure to do the assignment, I was prepared to make up a few up. Before the question-and-answer part of the day, Ostey announced that the day's topic would be menstruation and why this was significant as it related to a girl becoming a woman. He dimmed the lights in the room and began to show a short film reel that illustrated the subject in a bit more detail than apparently my flu-tainted stomach could handle. In grand fashion, I spewed all over the burnt orange carpet on the floor of the library.

Ostey and most of the class thought I had been grossed out by the subject matter, but the inspiration for my illness was not relevant.

The bottom line was I had to go home, in accordance with school rules, and miss Nativity vs. Holy Ghost. I didn't really feel sorry for saturating Mrs. Kingsley's carpet. After all, payback was fair play, and I hadn't forgotten that embarrassing announcement of hers. Still, the story of the boy who puked at PMS spread throughout school quickly, and I was the butt of more than a few jokes for a while, but I was able to laugh about it some myself.

As fate would have it, apparently there had been a segment about VD on the record I had never heard, and several questions were asked about it and answered after I went home the day I got sick. Sex education was a topic that absentees could not make up, so as far as I knew, French kissing Julie Hoffmann was a very risky adventure.

CHAPTER 41

Radio Lunchtime

In addition to getting drunk for the first time, my sixth grade year at Nativity School also included a few other deviant activities that are worthy of confessing. Perhaps among the most unscrupulous were what became a sometimes daily, and almost always a several-days-per-week delinquent indulgence: spending my lunch hours at the Oky Doky.

Lunchtime during my first five years at Nativity School revolved around walking the eight blocks from Nativity to 116, where we would be greeted by Great-Aunt Agnes, who had lunch on the table and ready to go, thus allowing us ample time to make the round-trip walk and eat within the allotted one hour. We could take Alpine Street, or we could take Nevada. The streets ran parallel to one another, and regardless of which one we chose, we could take them both straight home, all the way.

Part of what I remember about those early year lunch hours was the old-fashioned wooden box-style AM radio that sat on the counter behind Agnes' chair at the table. It had two big, black plastic knobs: One controlled the volume, and the other allowed for channel surfing, old school style. Agnes always had the old box tuned to station KDTH, 1370 on the AM dial. In many ways, the radio was like a verbal clock that paced and measured how long we had before we needed to be out the door and back to school. Every day, the news came on at the same time, was interrupted by the same commercials at the very same moment each day, and was followed by the weather and local obituary report. Agnes, then approaching ninety years old, seemed most attentive to the obituaries, as she often knew many of the names that were mentioned and did not want to miss the required prayer she must say for the deceased and their families. When the obituaries ended and the commercials for Rainbow Tire Company and Dubuque Packing Company meats were complete, it was time to fly.

The Dubuque Packing Company jingle sticks in my mind to this day because we must have heard it more than 1,000 times over those five years . . .

"D-U-B-U-Q-U-E spells Dubuque, the meat for your fam-i-ly, look for the bright red Fleu 'de lis, it's the symbol of flavor and qual-i-ty!"

If we were delayed into the start of the post-news listener call-in program *Sound Off*, with popular host Gordy Kilgore, we knew we would need to run part of the way back to school in order to avoid the late bell. We loved to listen to *Sound Off*, however, when we were off school in the summertime or when we stayed home from school sick because it was classic entertainment. In essence, it was the community 'get your bitch on the airwaves' show. The line was open for anyone to call in and complain to Gordy about whatever was in their craw that day. He would hear complaints ranging from, "Why was the trash picked up on Monday instead of Tuesday?" to "Gordy, don't ya think they should have a stoplight instead of a stop sign at Third and Main Streets?" Gordy did his best to follow up with the appropriate public officials or authorities and tried to get the common man his due justice. It was hilarious. Every single caller would begin their call by saying the exact same line, "Yeah, Gordy?" and would wait for him to say, "Yes" or "Go ahead. I'm here," before proceeding with their rant. Just once we wanted to hear Gordy reply with a smart-ass remark like, "Who the hell do you think I am, for Christ's sake? The Pope? Of course it's Gordy! It's always Gordy! What's your bitch?" but he never did because he was a public servant, a defender of the everyday Dubuque Schmo, and they all worshipped him. Surely it was the easiest time of day for the station sales manager to sell ad slots, as it was wildly popular, and Gordy was a local legend we all laughed at, but adored. Sometimes we would call in and make up a complaint just so we could hear our voice on the radio. For the Dubuquers who had the good fortune of getting their call past the always-busy switchboard and on the air, it became, as Andy Warhol described it, their fifteen minutes of fame.

My school lunch hour took a drastic change when I entered the sixth grade. That was the year my class began spending mornings in portable classrooms that resembled mobile homes and were placed on the grounds of the nearest public school, Lincoln, which was one long block to the south of Nativity. Because of the boom of large families with school-aged kids enrolled in Catholic schools, there was an overcrowding issue. The public school system agreed to take on the temporary burden of teaching Catholic kids at public schools for a few years, until the class sizes diminished. The deal was that the Nativity sixth graders had math, gym, and science from the public school curriculum in the morning at Lincoln and then walked over to Nativity at lunchtime for religion, social studies, and English in the afternoon. The Nativity fifth grade had their mornings at Nativity, and switched over to Lincoln in the afternoon. This kind of scheduling made use of Nativity's classrooms to the benefit of all involved and avoided the need for more schools to be built that would really not be needed after three or four years anyway. As practical and as financially prudent the solution was, I recall there being controversy among some of the nuns, priests, and parents at the time, upset at the thought of Catholic kids being taught in a non-religious environment. I guess even in the Church, however, whether anyone wanted to admit or not, money was not only the root of all evil, as was professed in the Bible, but it was also king—not to be confused with the King, who of course we all knew was Christ, despite what Elvis fans might have believed at the time.

CHAPTER 42

Oky Doky

Another controversy that was born of the student exchange program most directly impacted a man by the name of Ralph Grabow. In the grand scheme of things, it was Ralph who suffered the most from the Shared Time Program.

Ralph Grabow spent many years as a local barber. His vocation was a contradiction in career and identity, as he was totally bald and used a wax on his head that made it shine like the sun glistening off the Mississippi River on a hot summer afternoon. Perhaps even Ralph recognized the irony of what he had done for a living for about twenty years, because when Old Man McNamara retired and sold his goldmine of a candy and convenience store, located immediately across the street from Nativity School, Ralph tossed his barber smock, comb, and scissors into the garage sale his wife was having that Saturday and became a grocer merchant. Ralph bought McNamara's Market, closed it for a couple of months, did a little interior renovation, hung a new sign over the front doors to the place, and presto . . . Ralph's Oky Doky Mart. As with most other ideas, it seemed like a good one at the time.

For years, McNamara's was run efficiently and likely at a nice bottom line. During those years, there was no such thing as Shared Time, so no kids came into the store during the lunch hour, and students ventured into the Oky Doky only after school, a time when Old Man McNamara had the good sense to have several extra staff on hand to manage customer traffic and keep the crowd under surveillance.

Being new to the business, coupled with the new traffic flow at the lunch hour, caused by the commuting of students between Lincoln and Nativity, one might safely say Ralph faced a double handicap. Each school day, around twelve-thirty p.m., after we finished our lunch at Lincoln, about fifteen to twenty sixth graders would invade the Oky Doky at the same time. We perused the candy rack, which sat at one end of the store; the ice cream cooler, which was in another area; and the soda cooler, which was at yet one more area of the store. We carried book bags filled with books, of course, and duffle bags containing our gym clothes . . . or at least that is what the bags contained when we entered the Oky Doky. The contents upon leaving the store typically included candy bars, ice cream novelties, and sodas. The way it usually worked was that a group of us scattered to each of the three areas, and a couple guys would actually pick up some things and form a line at the register to occupy Ralph with ringing up the sales. As soon as we heard the register dinging and clinging, those of us at the various stations in the store would take turns stuffing the five-finger discount items in our bags. We cleaned old, bald, understaffed Ralph out almost on daily basis, but the poor guy could never really finger us because he was too busy ringing up the paying customers, accomplices that they were, to catch any of the various thieves in the act. He made pleas to the school, to which the most feared male teacher, Jim Osterberger, would respond to by keeping the entire class after school to lecture us on the sins some of us were committing and how severe the penalty would be if he ever caught any one of us in the act. We knew it was fifteen or twenty to one, and the odds were still stacked heavily against Ralph catching us, so the rip-offs continued.

To his credit, Ralph tried his best to remedy the problem. Pulling a page from the playbook of Old Man McNamara, Ralph hired another clerk to come in for a couple of hours during the mid-day hours, which allowed him to follow us around, keeping a close eye on our bags. He also instituted a policy to check bags at the door, only to be reclaimed upon leaving. Not easily dissuaded, we started stuffing things down our pants and in our coat pockets. Nothing short of a strip search policy or the nuclear option was going to stop us. Finally, after nearly a year of fun and games for us and what had to have been sheer agony for a struggling new entrepreneur, Ralph instituted a lunch hour ban on school kids in the store, which later was softened to only four of us at a time allowed in together. It began to become too much work, and too much risk, so the kleptomaniacs finally gave up. Apparently, it was a bit too late for Ralph, however, as he ended up selling the store to someone else shortly thereafter. All said, Ralph was a really nice man, and some of us felt pretty guilty about doing this to him and self-curtailed our activity long before others, but I won't mention any names, Kip.

CHAPTER 43

Shleets Slips Up

The red brick Schlueter family home sat one house removed from the corner of Alta Vista Street and Loras Boulevard. It was positioned dead center between Nativity School and Loras College and, as such, became a natural hangout and pitstop area for using the bathroom, warming ourselves, or grabbing a cup of hot chocolate when we were bouncing about the neighborhood during the winter season. Of the six Schlueter siblings, Jeff, who was a year behind me in school, was the one most connected to our group of Nativity guys from 1973 to 1975. Schleets was the fourth of six kids and was just entering the first grade at the time of his father's untimely loss to a battle with cancer. With the lack of success his parents were having with the rhythm method of birth control, as prescribed by the Catholic church, had Jeff's father lived, there might well have been another two or three Schlueter kids in the house before it was all said and done. Sad as it was for Schleets to lose his father when he did, it may have been just as well sooner than later perhaps, as Judy Schlueter's hands were already full enough with the crew she somehow managed to raise as a single parent for more of her life than not. Much like the Lyness brothers, the only kids we knew whose parents were divorced, the Schlueters were the only family we knew who had lost a parent before their natural time.

Although Shleets was in seventh grade when the rest of our gang was in eighth, he had the street smarts and daring of someone a few years older than us. With his mom working to support the family, busy running various kids around, and taking time now and then for herself to go out and enjoy an evening with her girlfriends, Jeff found a good deal of freedom to come and go as he pleased, though I'm not sure he always chose the best places to go or the best people to be with. Shleets seemed to get into more trouble than anyone other than Kipper, but they were pretty even, and many times, the two of them were together when the wrath of some authority figure at school or in the Nativity neighborhood had to help them see the errors of their ways. More often than not, that figure wound up being none other than James Paul Osterberger (JPO), the male role model and enforcer at Nativity who we learned to fear and idolize all in one. JPO, or Ostey as we also called him, entered the teaching profession fresh out of Loras College when most of our gang was in the fifth grade and Shleets was in the fourth. Ostey was among the first lay male teachers to enter the classroom ranks at the school, as the nuns who had ruled Nativity for so long began to dwindle in numbers. If the nuns were as tough as Marines, Ostey was more like the drill sergeant who put them through boot camp. The good sisters of The Visitation needed to lose no sleep wondering if there would be any loss of discipline or lightening of the rules as they turned over the reins to JPO. If anything, life at Nativity was about to get tougher.

Nativity School was separated into two distinct sections, connected by an enclosed walkway we called 'the bridge'. Those of us in the younger classes were in the old building, and the older classes, which included a lot of our older siblings, were in the new building. We had heard the horror stories regarding some of the things that went on in the new building under Ostey's rule, but although Ostey showed up at Nativity around 1971, it was actually several years later when most of us had our first real and regular experiences with him. The things we heard the first few years, however, were enough to send chills up our spines when we passed him in a common area of the school or out on the playground. We were hopeful that he would move on to another school by the time we went to the new building for sixth through eighth grades, but when we got there, Ostey was still teaching.

I recall an early January Saturday evening over Christmas break when 1974 turned to 1975. We had been out of school for about two weeks already and were scheduled to return the following Monday. At least on a subconscious level, we felt exempt from JPO's rules, because after all, what authority did he have over us when we were on break?

Most of the Loras College campus was deserted, as the college kids had returned to their hometowns for a month between winter and spring quarters. The exceptions were the basketball players, who had gone home for the holidays, but were required to return shortly after New Year's to resume practice in preparation for the start of conference play. It was not uncommon for a group of us from the Nativity gang to rebound for the Loras players when they practiced shooting or play a couple of the big guys two on three or four after practice was formally concluded. Because there was no game going on, the concession area was abandoned—no customers, no workers. There was simply a deserted Coca-Cola fountain, and Shleets was quick to spot it. As the Loras coaches and players retreated from the main level court area, down a couple flights of stairs to where the locker rooms and showers were located, a bad idea was born.

Shleets, Jungo, and Kip decided to disconnect the silver metal CO2 container hooked to the syrup hose and take it home with them. Their intent for it was anybody's guess, but in the blink of an eye, they had the heavy metal container loose and were dragging it out the front door of the Fieldhouse. Shleets's house was not far, and the sidewalks were a little icy, so they dragged and slid the container the block and a half to the Schlueter's garage. The plan was to hold the tank there temporarily until a more permanent location could be decided upon later that night. We needed to get into the house and warm up a bit and ponder the tank's final resting place, so we headed in, warmed some hot chocolate, and tuned the radio to

WDBQ so we could listen to some Top 40 hits and hang out for awhile.

We were sitting at the kitchen table, sipping our cocoa and listening to tunes, when WDBQ News Director Paul Hemmer, who broke in mid-song with a special report, interrupted our party in dramatic fashion. "Dubuque police have reported a murder at Marino's Meal on a Bun. While details are still evolving and police are on the scene, a customer reportedly walked into the sandwich shop earlier this evening, and after becoming suspicious when no employees could be found, opened the walk-in cooler and found that the clerk had been stabbed to death and left in the chilled area. Police advise citizens to stay home for the remainder of the evening and to lock your doors. Stay tuned to WDBQ Radio for details as they become available."

We were in shock and disbelief. There had never, ever been a murder in Dubuque to our knowledge—certainly not in our lifetimes. We were all pretty freaked out and began to close the shades over the windows of the house. Judy was not home, and we were not sure what to do. After fifteen or so minutes of huddling and pondering our next move, Kinger and I decided to pair up and make a break toward our homes together. We decided to take the same streets all the way, until he cut down Melrose Terrace and I continued the last two blocks down Alpine to Solon Street alone. We bid our buddies farewell and dashed off Shleets' porch in a sprint all the way home. When Kinger departed down Melrose and I was left to finish the last two blocks of my helter-skelter journey alone in the dark of the tainted night, I was as scared as I had ever been in my entire life.

The talk at school on the Monday, following a long holiday break, was usually about Christmas presents received, vacations taken, friends and relatives visited over the break, and other such things, but this time, the talk centered around what had happened at Marino's Meal on a Bun on Saturday night . . . and a silver metal CO2 tank that had somehow found its way to the office of Nativity School principal, Sister Patricia Clarke.

Although Sister Patricia was quite capable of handling disciplinary issues herself, she usually called JPO into the loop when the offenders were seventh or eighth grade boys. He knew our motives, he knew who usually associated with whom, and he could read through our lies and break us down like no one else. He was a real intimidating presence, the likes of which had never been seen at the school before.

As fate would have it, the mind-numbing distraction we experienced when the terrifying news report that hit the radio at Shleets' on Saturday night took all thoughts of the canister from our minds. As things turned out that night, we all split in different directions to flee a psycho killer on the loose and in the process had completely forgotten about the half of a soda dispenser. Apparently, Judy Schlueter pulled the car into the garage when she came home that night and stumbled upon it. When she could get no cooperation from any of her children as to where the mysterious item had come from, she called the school, knowing JPO could find the usual suspects and get to the bottom of the caper, which he did. Shleets, Yungo, and Kipper were all busted and suspended for the first two league basketball games of the new season. They were made to confess and make restitution to the Loras Booster Club, and were banned from the Loras campus for the rest of the school year. It was harsh, but everyone knew Ostey didn't mess around—even when murderers were on the loose.

CHAPTER 44

Ostey, Cos, Brownie and Alfie

Without question, Jim Osterberger was the patriarch of Nativity School. He ruled with an iron fist and was quick to brow beat, shake down, and even grab by the shirt collar and press against the wall with force any seventh or eighth grade boy who was foolish enough to doubt or challenge him. He gained our attention by instilling fear, but he gained our respect from his commitment to our growth and development as young men.

I recall a scene from the Nativity boys' locker room one day during the first week of football practice at the start of seventh grade. Ostey had come into the locker room to give us some type of motivational speech, along with some housekeeping things about the upcoming season. Included in his comments was an instruction that everyone needed to have a jock by the end of the week, and anyone who did not would be withheld from competition until he had fulfilled the requirement.

Stephen Frommelt, infamous for talking in class and not listening well and always rubbing Ostey the wrong way with his absentmindedness, had a look of absolute fright on his face. I told

Steve to relax and just go home and talk to his dad about it, and I was sure he could get Steve set up.

"Yeah, that's a good idea," he said. "I'll bet my dad can get me one of those."

Steve's father Paul was president of a family-owned company and was influential in the church and the Dubuque community as a whole. Certainly he could get this poor freaked-out kid a jock. I failed to understand the fear Steve had over the whole topic. Of course it could be a sensitive thing to purchase this type of thing for the first time, but the people at Zehtener's Sporting Goods dealt with this all the time. I didn't give it a second thought, and I didn't see why Steve should either.

The end of the week arrived, and there sat Steve after practice in the locker room, jockless, in his boxer shorts.

Ostey approached Steve and said, "Okay, Frommelt. You heard the rules, and once again, you have failed to comply. Don't come back until you've done what your teammates have all managed to accomplish."

"Tomorrow," Steve replied. "I start tomorrow."

"Sure," Ostey said. "I'll bet it won't be any different tomorrow."

"No, really," Steve said. "I told my dad, and he said I can work Saturday mornings at his company. I start tomorrow."

Ostey looked at Steve with a completely baffled expression and replied, "Frommelt, what the hell are you talking about?" His face turned red, as it always did when he was about to go off. The whole team was now tuned into the drama that was playing out before our eyes.

Steve was trembling, his eyes bigger than life. "You told us on Monday we had to have a job by the end of the week, and I got one. I just don't start until tomorrow."

"A jock, Frommelt! A jock. You know . . . an athletic support, nut cup, ball holder . . ."

The room burst into a fit of laughter. Everyone, including Ostey and Frommelt, could be heard two blocks away.

Although Ostey was persistent in outwardly positioning himself as the tough, dictatorial disciplinarian, there was a more supportive man inside the shell. That was the guy who inspired us with words of encouragement when the August heat was wearing our confidence thin during football conditioning drills, the guy who would invite a group of four or five of us to a homemade prime rib dinner at the vacation cottage he rented down at Massey Station, followed by games of Monopoly by the blazing rock fireplace, and the guy who took the same group canoeing and camping at the end of the school year as a way of demonstrating that he was not only a teacher, but also a mentor and friend.

On Saturdays, after our basketball season was over and the late winter and long thawing spring kept us indoors for another six to eight weeks, it was Ostey who would open the gym and join us in basketball pick-up games for half the day, just to be sure we had something constructive to do to wear us out so we wouldn't stay out too late on Saturday nights.

A couple of years after JPO came to Nativity; they brought in another young, single male role model named Mike Cosgrove. 'Cos', as we called him, was also fresh out of Loras College, where he had been a track star. Cos had a temper that would flare up only occasionally when we took too much advantage of his easygoing demeanor. Cos and Ostey became a good one-two combination. They complemented one another in their approach to dealing with us, kind of like the good cop/bad cop game policeman are trained to play in order to get the most out of someone they are interrogating.

While Ostey never seemed to have a serious girlfriend, Cos, on the other hand, did, and we were glad. Cos dated a woman by the name of Judy Wendt during his days at Loras, and the relationship carried over into the first few years he was at Nativity. When we took field trips to the YMCA/YWCA to go swimming or on the annual eighth grade picnic trip to Governor Dodge State Park and Lake in Wisconsin, there needed to be a female chaperone to attend to the girls in the locker rooms as they changed in and out of their swimwear. The first time Judy chaperoned the girls when we went to the Y to swim, she turned more than a couple of eighth-grade heads when she exited the locker room in her tight, bright yellow one-piece.

Judy was not heavy, but she was definitely full-figured and particularly well proportioned with curves in all the right places. She had brown curly hair, matching big brown eyes, and a beautiful toothpaste-commercial pearly white smile. The boys hoped Miss Wendt would accompany the girls on another swim outing, so we were all delighted when she appeared on board the Iowa Coaches charter bus that we all paid three dollars each to rent for our trip to Dodgeville, Wisconsin.

The eighth-grade trip the week after graduation was a traditional rite of passage for Nativity students turned alumni. After eight years of grade school together, this would be our last time as a group before some of us would be going separate ways to different high schools. We packed picnic lunches, watermelons, and a giant cooler of soda. Ostey, Cos, Judy, and a couple of parents were our guides. The first order of business upon arrival at the state park was to hit the dressing rooms and then head down to the sandy beach for some volleyball. The boys were all in and out of the beach house dressing rooms in no time, and we were on the sand checking out the girls as they exited the dressing rooms. While they were cute, they were relatively undeveloped girls, with the exception of Nancy Gearhardt, who had woman boobs from about the sixth grade on. We waited patiently for Miss Wendt to step out in the Miss America-style one-piece we all thought she looked pretty good in at the Y back in February, but none of us could have imagined what we were about to see.

When Cos's girl walked out of the ladies' dressing room in a navy blue two-piece bikini with white polka dots shakin' her God-given assets, every boy on the beach just stared and drooled. Jungo got so excited that his anatomy below the waist began to grow at a rapid rate, giving him no option but to dive immediately into the water, where he had to remain for about twenty minutes until he could return to the sand without fear of embarrassing himself. Even Cos noticed the effect Judy's suit—or more so, what was revealed by it—was having on so many of the boys, so much to our dismay, she ended up putting on a t-shirt to achieve a bit more modesty. We didn't think the t-shirt was necessary, but I guess the parents who came along did.

Dave Brown was a college student who lived a few blocks from Nativity and had aspirations of being a football coach. When I was in the fifth grade, I remember him coaching my brother Tom, at the quarterback position, but shortly thereafter, 'Brownie' sort of disappeared without much notice. Three years later, at the start of eighth grade, I walked onto the football field for the first day of practice, helmet in hand, and noticed we had a new coach. The guy had long brown hair, as long as a girl's, and wore a green official Army military shirt cut off at the sleeves with the last name 'BROWN' stitched above the pocket on the left side.

With little fanfare, Brownie had been sent on a three-year hiatus to Southeast Asia, Vietnam, to be specific, compliments of Uncle Sam. He was back to coach the offense for our eighth-grade season, and while we were thrilled to see him, the dramatic physical change in appearance, along with a far more thoughtful, reflective, and overall mellower demeanor took some adjustment on our part.

Brownie was great. He was one of those guys who always had something uplifting to say about everyone. He was an instant dose of self-esteem for those of us who followed him around like he was the Pied Piper. Dave re-enrolled at the University of Wisconsin-Platteville, this time on the GI bill, and made sure his class schedule allowed him time to make the thirty-minute drive back to Dubuque in time for Nativity Royals football practice.

Brownie worked the Saturday evening cash register/clerk slot at the Oky Doky. When he worked, we went in there to talk to him for two or three hours. We couldn't get enough. He was a big Joe Namath fan and often wore the Number 12 New York Jets jersey to his job at the store. If Ralph Grabow wanted to put an end to the lunchtime theft from the start, all he needed to do was put Coach Brown on that shift. We respected him too much to ever even think of stealing when he was there. Heck, we would have mopped the floor and stocked the shelves if he had asked us to. We respected the man that much.

We had some very good and positive male role models at Nativity, and their investments in us, as inconsequential as they may have seemed at the time, played a critical role in helping us to become the responsible and contributing members to society that most of us turned out to be. We could never adequately thank them for all they gave us, but years later, they and we know their efforts were obviously well placed. An equally important female figure in our lives, Gail Alfredo, taught our homeroom class at the Lincoln School shared time program. She always had time for us socially, but challenged us academically and could throw down discipline right up there with Ostey. She was special to all of us.

CHAPTER 45

Graduation

Two days before our eighth grade graduation, I was called into the Principal's Office. When I arrived, I must have looked afraid or nervous, which I was. Sister Patricia Clarke put me at ease and told me to relax. She just had a favor to ask of me. It seemed there was a need for about four boys to stay after school on the second-to-last day to assist Father O'Brien at the rectory, attending to a few tasks he and the other priests needed help with. Sister P. asked if I would help and find three other guys who would join me. I told her I would, and I did. I grabbed Kipper, Kinger, and Jungo, and together we spent about thirty minutes helping with some manual labor at the rectory. That was it, or so I thought—a simple favor asked, a simple favor done.

Graduation night came, and our entire class of about forty-five, decked out in dresses and leisure suits, led a procession into the church, followed by our families, to the playing of the church organ. We walked down the aisle proudly, memories flashing from so many chapters of our lives that somehow connected to this building, the House of the Lord. There were some memories we would have been embarrassed to admit to, but they still brought smiles to our faces.

After we were seated and participated in our last official school Mass, Sister Patricia walked to the microphone placed near the pulpit on the altar. She began by saying that the class of 1975 was filled with many great young people who would go far in life and do great service to the Church in the shadow of the Lord. Then she shared that it was time to announce the recipients of the American Legion Citizenship Awards, one to the outstanding boy citizen/ leader and one to the outstanding girl.

As Connie Alt was invited up to the altar to be recognized as the female recipient, I wondered whom, with all the unscrupulous dealings this class of boys had been a party to, could be selected. When Connie walked back to her seat proudly holding her golden certificate, Sister Patricia began to tell a story of how, two days prior, she had administered, a secret test to the boy who had been selected. We all wondered what she was talking about until she began to expose a tale about making up a story involving priests needing a helping hand. Things began to unravel as Sister P. told the congregation how she had used the request for a favor as one last test to see if the boy was worthy of the award and that the recipient came through just as she had witnessed so many times before. I was in shock. My immediate thoughts revolved around the incredible guilt I felt for having done so many sneaky things in and around the school over the years. Then, as she invited me forward to receive the award and I turned back and viewed my competition, I concluded that she might have a point.

As the graduating Nativity School Class of 1975 prepared to go on to the next phase of life, which we were told would be far less sheltered and protected than our years at the Catholic school had been, we were encouraged to use the guiding principles we had been taught to steer a straight path when life's twists and turns tried to derail us. Somehow, as we reflected on the secret crossroads we had already negotiated over the previous eight years within our families, at school, and in our neighborhoods that few of our parents, mentors, and teachers in the audience had any knowledge of, we felt pretty good about our chances of survival going forward. If they only knew . . . and I guess now they do!